GOOD MONEY

JONATHAN SELF is a journalist and entrepreneur, and the author of *Self Abuse, The Teenager's Guide to Money, Honey's Natural Feeding Handbook for Dogs* and *Emerald: Twenty-one Centuries of Jewelled Opulence and Power.*

GOOD MONEY

MONEY

BECOME AN ETHICAL ENTREPRENEUR

CHANGE THE WORLD

FEEL BETTER

JONATHAN SELF

HEAD
ZEUS

First published in the UK in 2017 by Head of Zeus Ltd

9 7 5 3 1 2 4 6 8

A catalogue record for this book is available from
the British Library.

'Joe Heller' by Kurt Vonnegut originally published in
The New Yorker. © Kurt Vonnegut LLC. Used by permission.

ISBN (HB) 9781786691163
ISBN (E) 9781786691248

Typeset by Adrian McLaughlin

Printed and bound in Great Britain by
CPI Group (UK) Ltd, Croydon CR0 4YY

Head of Zeus Ltd
First Floor East
5–8 Hardwick Street
London EC1R 4RG

WWW.HEADOFZEUS.COM

For Rose

CONTENTS

INTRODUCTION
MAKE A DIFFERENCE

YOU know what Ralph Waldo Emerson said: 'If a man can build a better mousetrap than his neighbours, though he builds his house in the woods, the world will make a beaten path to his door.'

It turns out to be true for dog food, too. I can't think of any way to make what I am about to say sound anything other than fatheaded, but my friend Vicky Marshall and I created a better dog food (admittedly by accident), did nothing to promote it, put obstacles in the way of customers who wanted to buy it and the world still made a beaten path to our door. Well, maybe not an actual beaten path, but the small, artisan dog food company we founded is successful by any measure you care to choose: turnover, employee numbers, profitability, publicity or influence.

I am delighted to say (it being peopled for the most part by callous, avaricious, dishonest, thoughtless hypocrites) that the entire pet food industry has been shaken up a bit by Honey's Real Dog Food. We have had lots of newspaper and magazine articles written about us, we're referenced in several books, and what we do was the subject of a television documentary. Unusually for a business, Honey's has no sales function. We are happy to show people how they can make the same food themselves so that they don't have to become our customers. We provide unlimited, free canine nutrition and health advice (supplied by in-house veterinary professionals) to anyone who contacts us.

Other things make the company stand out. Our stated objectives are to educate consumers about canine welfare and campaign against speciesism. We use ingredients that are suitable for human consumption, visit all the producers from whom we buy our meat to make sure they treat their animals and birds with genuine compassion, donate 1 per cent of our sales to a charity that fights for higher standards of farm animal welfare, and support any good cause that approaches us.

A BUSINESS FOCUSED
ALMOST ENTIRELY ON
IMPROVING
SOME ASPECT OF
THE WORLD
WE LIVE IN,
RATHER THAN ON
FINANCIAL GAIN,
CAN NOT ONLY
HELP TO ACHIEVE
POSITIVE,
MEANINGFUL
CHANGE, BUT
WILL ALSO GENERATE
ABOVE-AVERAGE
PROFITS.

We started Honey's with a few thousand pounds of our own money and we have no outside investors or bank loans. Incidentally, I have never had any day-to-day involvement in the business.

The reason I am writing this book is to show, by example, that a business focused almost entirely on improving some aspect of the world we live in, rather than on financial gain, can not only help to achieve positive, meaningful change, but will also generate above-average profits. It summarizes a lifetime's business experience into something you can read in a couple of hours.

If you are planning to start a new business, I hope to persuade you to think in terms of how it can achieve some higher goal. If you own an existing business (or you are an investor or an employee), I hope to persuade you to alter its direction so that social responsibility becomes its new priority. There is ample evidence that genuinely ethical businesses are less likely to fail and more likely to be sustainable. They also return higher shareholder value – in terms of cash and in terms of satisfaction.

What global concerns do you have? For my own part I have a long list of worries, not least the damage humans are doing to the natural environment, the suffering endured by the poor, the plight of migrants, the growing number of countries without democratically elected governments, the rise of extremism, gender inequality and the appalling cruelty that mankind inflicts daily upon untold billions of animals, birds and fish.

Traditionally, society has looked to its politicians and public servants to make improvements and correct wrongs. The main way in which we, as individuals, could influence what happened was by voting or making some other public demonstration. The growth of the consumer society has altered all of that. How people spend their money can have more effect nowadays than how they vote.

Businesses that ignore consumer sentiment are taking a terrible risk, whereas businesses that empower consumers are opening themselves to opportunity. Humans can be selfish and short term in their thinking. But they can also show moral capacity, compassion and a desire for justice. When you set up an ethical business, you tap into the best of human nature. You and your customers are joined in a mutual desire to make a difference.

HOW I GOT INTO
ETHICAL DOG FOOD

I never set out to launch an ethical business. It happened like this. On and off throughout my life I have been involved with farming. My father reported on agriculture for the *Economist* and *The Times* and wrote a book called *The State and the Farmer* and I was making farm visits before I could walk. In my late teens, I had a brief career selling warm water udder washers into dairy farms. Longing to try farming for myself, I bought what the locals referred to dismissively as a 'hobby farm' in Australia on which I ran cattle and sheep. Later, in Ireland, I obtained twenty pigs to clear a walled garden – because pigs are a sort of organic Agent Orange and I didn't want to use weedkiller.

These pigs were not, it transpired, practising safe sex, and before I knew it I had over a hundred piglets on my hands.

I could write a separate book about my life with those pigs. They were extremely healthy on account of their outdoor existence and the fact that I never allowed anyone onto the farm who could possibly introduce disease. Actually, the only thing the pigs ever suffered from (weirdly, given the Irish weather) was sunburn. I solved this by the judicious application of Ambre Solaire and have often wondered since if families were saying to each other over the Sunday roast: 'Does this crackling taste like suntan lotion to you? It does to me.'

The pigs were extraordinarily intelligent and I was able to organize them into two soccer teams – although I could never get any of them to understand the offside rule. I was surprised to find that they had a sense of humour. One of the sows, for example, used to sneak up behind me and stick her snout between my legs so that I would topple over. This caused all the pigs to – and there is no other word for it – cackle.

Anyway, I am digressing. The point I want to make is that almost immediately after the piglets were born, it dawned on me that they would have to be slaughtered.

There is no perfect way to kill a living creature, but it is obviously better if it is unexpected, quick and painless. Pigs like their own personal space and find being confined with a lot of other pigs stressful. Hugh Fearnley-Whittingstall recommends feeding one's pigs in a trailer and then driving them around a field in it so that when the time comes to take them to the abattoir they aren't frightened by the journey. He also suggests getting them drunk beforehand. Inspired, I did a test run with a pair of sows who (thanks to a couple of bottles of stout) were virtually singing sea shanties on the way to the local butcher.

I hated the experience but felt that inebriating the pigs was the least bad of the available options. It transpired that the butcher, an elderly man, could take only one or two pigs a month and it seemed that most of the piglets would die of old age long before he could dispatch them. Reluctantly, I sold the whole herd for a pittance to an organic farmer who eventually sent them, packed into a crowded transporter, to a slaughterhouse some two hours' drive away.

As a result of my experience with the pigs, I gave up farming livestock and became a vegetarian. My rationale for this can be summed up by something George Bernard Shaw said: 'Animals are my friends... and I don't eat my friends.' In time, I came to understand that there are other powerful arguments for vegetarianism. The environmental cost of eating meat and fish is enormous. Moreover, humans were originally herbivores and if we follow a wholefood, plant-based diet we seem to lead longer, healthier lives. As I have studied the subject it has become increasingly evident to me that it would be better for us and our planet if we all became vegetarians and – ideally – vegans.

Just because it would be better for us and our planet, however, doesn't mean it would be better for our four-legged companions. Dogs are carnivores. Over thousands of years, humans have altered the external appearance of dogs through selective breeding, but from an anatomical perspective they are identical to grey wolves. The two subspecies are so closely related that they can interbreed. What do wolves and wild dogs eat? Prey. They have the capacity to catch, kill, eat and digest it. The species-appropriate diet for a dog is raw meat, raw bone (yes, they can digest bone) and a certain amount of raw fruit and vegetable. This is what man's best friend was fed prior to the invention of processed dog food in the 1860s.

MANY ETHICAL BUSINESSES HAVE **AN ACCIDENTAL QUALITY** TO THEM.

Processed dog food then, and now, is made using waste ingredients unsuitable for human consumption (rotten meat, poor-quality grain and so forth). It is unimaginably profitable and for over 150 years manufacturers have laboured to persuade dog owners in developed countries that it is the best possible diet for Fido and Fifi. However, from the 1930s onwards, dissenting voices began to be heard. A handful of biologists, zoologists and veterinary surgeons pointed out that dogs lived longer, healthier lives on a natural, 'raw' diet. By the start of the new millennium, what became known as the biologically appropriate raw food movement (it has the unfortunate acronym BARF), although far from mainstream, was starting to gain traction. My own vet, Tom Farrington, was a supporter.

Tom tried to persuade me to switch my dogs to a raw food diet. I considered him an extremely good vet. He had ministered to my chickens, goats, pigs and horses, as well as to the dogs and cats of the house, with wonderful results. But on the subject of feeding raw chicken wings and similar to dogs we parted company. I thought he was mad. My house-sitter, on the other hand, was taken with the idea and, while I was away, switched all the dogs to Tom's recommended diet. At the time,

I was fostering dogs and there were always six or seven in residence, and I returned to find a pack of extremely happy hounds. Raw marrowbones, duck carcasses, tripe and pork ribs were – apparently – just what they had always wanted.

I hadn't the heart to switch them back to dry processed food, but, having become a vegetarian, I found preparing their food stomach-churning. I searched for a company that made a complete raw food using ethically sourced ingredients. None existed. As it happened, Vicky and I had been planning an altogether different business – a financial services website – over the course of the previous year, but had just decided to chuck it in. I expected Vicky to laugh at me when I proposed that we become artisan dog food producers. In fact, she had just read an article on the subject and thought the idea was worth exploring.

Interestingly, many ethical businesses seem to have a similar, accidental quality to them. Jeffrey Hollender, founder of Seventh Generation, which produces plant-based cleaning products, was searching for an environmentally sensitive alternative to harsh, chemical detergents. Ian Rosenberger, founder of Thread International, which turns waste plastic into clothing fabric, was distressed by the poverty and rubbish he saw in Haiti. Safia Minney, founder of fashion label People Tree, was fed up with the fact that Fair Trade clothing was of poor quality and looked (not that she has ever put it this way) like it was made from sacking.

KNOW THYSELF

YOU don't have to be young. You don't have to work at it every hour of the night or day. You don't have to be interested in money. But if you are starting a business, any sort of a business, you must have a good understanding of your strengths and weaknesses, likes and dislikes.

I was middle-aged when Honey's was conceived. Then, as now, I earned the majority of my living as a writer. I led a fairly peripatetic existence and worked every day of the year, from home or – to be more precise – wherever I happened to be. My priority was spending time with my children, who lived in Australia and Britain, and caring for my adopted mother, who was then ninety-six and lived in America.

Vicky was in an altogether different position. For starters, she had a proper career, being something terrifically important in the marketing department at Nationwide Building Society. Also, she was married with three much younger children. The Marshalls lived in a beautiful rural part of Wiltshire. Vicky had taken a year of unpaid leave to launch our financial services website and when we decided to close it down, she asked herself whether the massive salary she would receive if she returned to work at Nationwide was truly worth the sacrifices it would entail.

We divided the various tasks and responsibilities required to get Honey's off the ground between us, taking into account our skills, personalities and locations. My primary role was to come up with the ideas, establish the principles by which we would operate, devise the business model and write all the communication material. In a nutshell, I was (with Vicky's input, of course) to provide the vision. I was able to do my Honey's work at almost any hour of the day or night and from anywhere in the world. Vicky handled everything else. That is to say: running the office, looking after the customers, finding the ingredients, overseeing the manufacturing, arranging the deliveries, handling the finance, supervising the staff, dealing with

YOU CAN'T FAKE
**MORAL
CONCERNS.**
OR, RATHER, YOU
CAN, BUT YOU'LL
QUICKLY BE
UNCOVERED AS
A FRAUD.

suppliers, meeting the regulations, and generally managing things.

When we started she was able to do this from home. Indeed, for the first two years, her house served as our offices, kitchens, packing room and storage space. No company, to my mind, flourishes with two bosses, so we agreed that Vicky would have total autonomy. I would stay well away from the actual business.

One of the reasons why businesses fail is that their founders haven't taken the time to analyse themselves. Vicky would have absolutely no problem developing a successful business concept. I like to think that if push came to shove, I could just about run Honey's without her. We find, however, that we both work much better in partnership. We have complementary skills, play to one another's strengths and share the same values. I would trust Vicky with my life.

In planning a business, it is vital to consider what you are good and bad at as well as what you love and hate. The Roman poet Juvenal put it well:

Yes, know thyself: in great concerns or small,
Be this thy care, for this, my friend, is all.

The need for self-awareness is even greater when

it comes to an ethical business. If you have to force yourself to care and/or if you are motivated predominantly by thoughts of wealth, my advice is: don't bother. You can't fake moral concerns. Or, rather, you can, but you'll quickly be uncovered as a fraud. Ethical consumers shun businesses that pretend to be something they are not, even more than they shun businesses that have no regard for the consequences of their actions.

A QUICK ASIDE

BEFORE I say anything else, I feel I ought to quickly explain what Honey's actually does. We make it easy for our customers to feed their dogs a species-appropriate diet – that is to say, the sort of diet dogs would eat in the wild, which would largely be prey – without having to introduce animal or bird carcasses into the home. Dogs are no different from humans (or any other animal, for that matter) and thrive when fed the correct food.

We offer around thirty different recipes, all made with certified organic, wild or free-range meat, sourced in the UK and suitable for human consumption. As bone ought to account for about a third of a dog's nutrition, we grind it up very small so that it can barely be seen. The food is raw and packaged in 'shires', which gives it the appearance of salamis or black puddings. After it has been made it is frozen and sent to customers by overnight courier. We also offer meaty bones (nature's toothbrushes) and other ingredients for customers who want to prepare their own food (which saves about a third of the cost).

We provide unlimited advice on raw feeding as well as recipes and support to anyone who asks us – there is no need to become a customer. We employ a Health Team, including vets and veterinary nurses, to provide free advice for poorly dogs. All our feeding recommendations are tailor-made so as to take into consideration the dog's health, weight, gender, lifestyle and likes and dislikes. Most of our customers order monthly and around 98 per cent of all sales are made to repeat customers. Honey's only sells direct and cannot be purchased in shops.

ANY IDEA IS ONLY AS GOOD AS ITS EXECUTION

THE core concept on which any enterprise is founded is, of course, of vital importance. However, ideas are of extremely limited value. Thrive Store, an American e-commerce, membership-based retailer, is founded on a very simple premise: cut out the middleman and supply healthy food (especially organic and non-GM food) direct to customers at an affordable price. Its founders wanted to counter the geographic and financial barriers that prevent most consumers from eating well. Its success ($120m turnover in its third year of operation) relies on an unquantifiable number of factors from efficient management to adequate funding and from the owners' motivation to their negotiating skills. So, although this book is largely concerned with ethical business ideas, I want to stress that any idea is only as good as its execution.

NOT CUSTOMERS, FELLOW TRAVELLERS

TWO years after we launched Honey's, we discovered that we were losing money on most of the orders. This is because, wanting to be egalitarian, I had worked out a pricing structure that involved charging a month's supply of food at cost plus £20 per dog. The £20 was to cover all our overheads and profit. The pricing formula was incredibly difficult to calculate and, it transpired, not especially fair since it meant the owners of small dogs were paying us disproportionately more than the owners of large dogs. Also, we couldn't tell our customers what our food actually cost. Frankly, in a lifetime of coming up with stupid ideas, it was one of my worst.

Vicky had said from the outset that she thought my pricing strategy was unfeasible, but in the face of my unwavering confidence had, reluctantly, agreed. You don't expect to make a profit when you start a business, which is why it took so long for my idiocy to become apparent. Once it did, we devised a new, simpler pricing structure that also took into account the rising cost of ingredients (we were in a market where free-range chicken was going up by 5 per cent a month!). We wrote to our customers and explained what had happened. In most cases, it meant an increase in price; in other cases, it meant a reduction. We promised to phase the new prices in over several months. To our surprise, we didn't receive a single complaint. In fact, a sizeable proportion of our customers offered to pay the new prices immediately and some even offered to pay us a 'bonus' to make up for our losses.

Honey's customers do not perceive themselves as being in a commercial relationship with the company. They see themselves as being fellow travellers. They believe, as we do, in species-appropriate diets for dogs, better farm animal welfare and higher standards of environmental care. I am willing to bet that we share other things in common: a hatred of big business, for example,

OUR CUSTOMERS DO NOT PERCEIVE THEMSELVES AS BEING IN A COMMERCIAL RELATIONSHIP WITH THE COMPANY. THEY **SEE THEMSELVES** AS BEING **FELLOW TRAVELLERS**.

and a desire to support small-scale British farming. I know – because we have a close relationship with them – that our customers are principled, honest, decent, kind, generous people. They knew that we wouldn't take advantage of them by putting up prices for the sake of it.

Socially responsible businesses, then, attract terrifically nice customers who share the owners' values. They also attract terrifically nice suppliers and employees. I am spiritual (or maybe just superstitious, who knows?) as opposed to religious, but I have noticed that when we need something at Honey's it often materializes from nowhere. As the Bible says (Matthew 7:7): 'Ask, and it shall be given you; seek, and ye shall find; knock, and it shall be opened unto you.'

To offer you just two examples of this (and I could provide you with hundreds):

When we were looking for our own premises, the perfect commercial kitchen became available, rent-free for three years, a few minutes' drive from Vicky's house.

We don't have to spend a penny on advertising as a steady flow of customers has come to us through word of mouth.

Never in my working life have things fallen into place as easily as they have with Honey's. We have made our mistakes and had our problems, but at every turn we seem to have been blessed with good fortune. My best guess, and I am really trying hard to rein in my inner hippie, is that it follows from pursuing some higher goal. It is, by the way, a humbling experience.

THE MONEY DOES FOLLOW

SOCIALLY responsible businesses achieve better sales, generate better profits and fare better during times of economic turmoil. I know this from personal experience, but there is plenty of independent research on the subject:

- In 2008, **Price Waterhouse Cooper** said: 'There is a positive, statistically significant, linear association between sustainability and corporate financial performance.'

- An **Economist Intelligence Unit** report ('Corporate Citizenship: Profiting from a sustainable business', 2008) said that seven out of ten business leaders believed ethical business behaviour helped increase profits.

• In 'The Economics and Politics of Corporate Social Performance' (2009), the authors, David P. Baron, Maretno A. Harjoto and Hoje Jo, found that: 'Greater corporate social performance is associated with better corporate financial performance.'

• In 2009, the Social Enterprise Coalition published research showing that, even though the UK was in recession, six out of ten social enterprises had seen their turnover increase compared to three out of ten businesses in general.

• In 2012, the International Finance Corporation found that the Dow Jones Sustainability Index (companies that put sustainability first) performed an average of 36.1 per cent better than the traditional Dow Jones Index.

• In 2013, Harvard Business School said that: 'High sustainability companies significantly outperform their counterparts over the long term, both in terms of stock market as well as accounting performance.'

- **A meta-analysis of corporate social responsibility** that covered a sample size of 33,878 observations...

... But I am labouring the point. There is no doubt, however, that socially responsible businesses are more successful. But the money doesn't 'follow' for just anything. You have to have a feasible business idea and you have to execute it well.

One of the reasons why this is true is because the people who own, run, work for, buy from and supply an ethical business have so much tied up in its success. If Honey's were to fail, my stakeholders and I would be losing more than money, jobs, dog food or custom. We would be losing a dream. We are attempting to change the way food producers – especially, dog food producers – think and operate. We are trying to help the unimaginable numbers of animals who experience dreadful fear and pain every day as a result of mankind's cruelty. We are intellectually and emotionally engaged with what we are doing. We need Honey's to survive and prosper so that we can pursue our larger agenda.

As an aside, I would be delighted if all the other dog food producers decided to operate to our standards and squeezed us out of the market. To my mind, Honey's doesn't have a single genuine

SOCIALLY
RESPONSIBLE
BUSINESSES
ACHIEVE
**BETTER
SALES,**
GENERATE
**BETTER
PROFITS** AND
FARE BETTER
DURING TIMES OF
ECONOMIC TURMOIL.

competitor. No other dog food producer in the world, let alone in the UK, puts as much effort into farm animal welfare, ingredient quality, education, research and customer service. I only wish they did. We have actually invited other manufacturers in to see what we do in the hope that they would emulate us, but to no avail.

Consumers are not only loyal to socially responsible businesses but also happy to pay a higher price for a product or service that they perceive as being more ethical. I feel I have quoted enough research in this section already, but if you want to know more, search online for a study conducted by the *Wall Street Journal* in 2008. Unfortunately, some businesses have no compunction when it comes to exploiting their more moral customers. A good example of this is coffee shop chains that charge a substantial premium for Fairtrade coffee but do not pass the extra profit on to the coffee growers. Happily, such companies are invariably found out and pay a price for their lying. McKinsey, the management consultants, discovered that almost one in ten American consumers had stopped shopping in Walmart because they were upset over things they had heard about the company. The Co-operative Group's 'Ethical Consumer Markets Report' suggests that half of all consumers will avoid a product or company with a poor reputation.

Another thing. The concept of 'reduce, recycle, reuse' is close to every socially responsible entre-preneur's heart. We hate waste and this translates into leaner (but obviously not meaner) businesses. I can offer you a practical example. You may have noticed that it is possible to buy free-range or organic chicken breasts and thighs in your local supermarket. Once these have been removed from the carcass it becomes almost valueless, because no one wants to cook a chicken with these essential bits missing. Dogs, however, couldn't care less. So, at Honey's we buy all the free-range and organic chicken carcasses we can get our paws on. It means they aren't thrown away and it saves us money (which is reflected in our prices). Ethical businesses tend to be streamlined and efficient, which translates into a higher return on capital.

Finally, a business that is intent on creating a better tomorrow is, as a matter of course, focused on the future. Its managers are planning and investing with the long term in mind. Such an approach ensures the business is more robust.

HOW TO RECOGNIZE AN 'ETHICAL BUSINESS'

I am conscious that I have been bandying about the terms 'ethical business' and 'socially responsible business' without actually spelling out what I mean.

Businesses wield power – the power, amongst other things, to control and exploit resources, create employment, transfer wealth and influence human behaviour. In most respects, a company's power is linked to its size, but there are exceptions. Small businesses, individually and collectively, can, for example, have a major effect on what people think and do. As proof of this one only has to study the green movement, which started at the grass-roots level and has always been closely linked with alternative, artisanal businesses.

With power, of course, comes responsibility. The responsibility, amongst other things and not necessarily in this order, to generate a profit for investors, care for staff, obey the law, be a good force in the community and protect the natural world. Ethical businesses understand this and consider what impact they have on their shareholders, employees, suppliers and customers, as well as on society as a whole, the environment and future generations. More than this, they use the power of business (I simply can't think of a better term to express what I mean) in order to solve social and/or environmental problems. The best way to explain this is, perhaps, with some examples:

Blake Mycoskie, a young American entre-preneur, was distressed by the sight of children without shoes while on a trip to Argentina. At the same time, he noticed that the Argentinians produced an inexpensive canvas shoe called the *alpargata*. He came up with the idea of importing *alpargatas* into the USA and giving a pair away to someone who was shoeless for every pair sold. He called the concept 'one for one' (other businesses have since adopted it) and the company Tomorrow's Shoes, or Toms. To date, Toms has given away sixty million pairs of shoes.

Warby Parker makes fashionable prescription glasses. For every pair the company sells at full price, it sells another pair for a nominal price (to avoid contributing to a culture of dependency) to someone in need. To date, it has (a) trained and employed hundreds of opticians in poorer countries, and (b) distributed over two million pairs of glasses to people who would otherwise be unable to see properly.

Dr. Bronner's – a family-owned, billion-dollar, organic skincare and toiletries manufacturer – creates environmentally friendly products and 'uses the profits to make a better world'. In 1929, its founder, a German soap-maker called Emanuel Bronner, wanted to spread a message of world peace, which he called his Moral ABC. To get people to come to his lectures, he started giving away free bars of soap and then he hit on the idea of printing his message on the soap wrapper. There is a company rule that the highest-paid member of staff will never earn above five times more than the lowest-paid (the average for US public companies is 204 times!).

Rubies in the Rubble is fighting food waste with relish! (Their pun, not mine.) The company creates jams and chutneys from surplus fruit and vegetables taken for free from wholesale markets. Its main aim is to bring attention to the fact that in the UK a third of all food and drink is thrown away. As an aside, the company has a policy of trying to give jobs to the long-term unemployed.

Divine Chocolate make divine chocolate – over fifty different types. The company was started as a joint venture with Body Shop, Twin Trading (an NGO that believes in development through trade) and a cocoa farming cooperative in Ghana called Kuapa Kokoo (now the largest shareholder). The company pays its producers well above the market price and also returns almost half its profits to community projects.

Fairphone is a new smartphone made using conflict-free materials (such as gold, tin, tantalum and tungsten) in a factory that pays its workers well. The mobile phone industry is one of the least ethical in the world and the company, which recognizes that it still has development work to do, wishes to bring this important issue to the public's attention.

Belu, a bottled mineral water, gives all its profits (£1.5m to date) to WaterAid, which creates clean water supplies for people in poorer countries.

Patagonia, the outdoor clothing and equipment company, has as its mission statement: 'To build the best product, cause no unnecessary harm, use business to inspire and implement solutions to the environmental crisis.' Its founders, who are amateur mountain climbers, donate over 1 per cent of sales to grass-roots environmental groups and the company's products are designed to reduce environmental impact.

There is, incidentally, a marked difference between an ethical business and a business that has a corporate and social responsibility (CSR) policy. Some CSR is carried out from the best of motives and has a truly beneficial impact. Sadly, though, a great deal of CSR is undertaken for purely commercial reasons. Society expects big

Ethical

ENTERPRISES USE
THE POWER OF
BUSINESS IN ORDER
TO **SOLVE**
SOCIAL
AND / OR
ENVIRONMENTAL
PROBLEMS.

businesses in particular to give back and donations have the added advantage of being tax deductible. Those engaged in less than ethical industries – such as defence, oil, gas, mining, tobacco, alcohol, gambling, insurance, automobiles and pharmaceuticals – may also use their CSR budget to create an entirely erroneous impression of their activities.

The World Land Trust, of which I was a trustee for many years, was frequently offered substantial donations by businesses that wanted their customers and the media to believe they were mindful of the environment. A retail supermarket chain, for example, tempted us with a million-pound-plus sponsorship deal if we would endorse one of its food lines. This would have meant overlooking any amount of dubious corporate behaviour, not least the sale of live turtles in China. We declined, but doubtless it found another not-for-profit organization willing to take its money.

There is a trend, particularly amongst public companies, to produce an annual CSR report. These are, almost without exception, self-serving. When genuinely ethical companies are talking to their stakeholders they openly discuss the challenges they face, the difficulty of measuring success, why and where they are failing and how they intend to do better. Patagonia, for example, is open about the problems it faces: 'We know that our business activity – from lighting stores to dyeing shirts – creates pollution as a by-product. So we work steadily to reduce those harms.'

WHY I AM AN ETHICAL, NOT A SOCIAL ENTREPRENEUR

THERE'S another term that gets used a great deal, that of 'social entrepreneur'.

A social entrepreneur is someone who employs business techniques to develop, fund and implement solutions to social, cultural or environmental issues, but without a profit motive.

Some social entrepreneurs have never really been involved in business. Others have had long and successful commercial careers. Indeed, many of the best-known social entrepreneurs, such as Bill Gates, Chuck Feeney and George Soros, became extremely wealthy before they turned to philanthropic work.

Confusingly, some ethical entrepreneurs are also social entrepreneurs. That is to say, they are involved in one or more ethical business ventures and they also use their business skills and acumen for different, not-for-profit purposes.

Even if I was wealthy enough not to have to work, I am not sure that I would want to switch from being an ethical to a purely social entrepreneur. It is true that there is a strong element of self-interest in ethical business (the sense of doing good and making money at the same time) but maybe this is what makes it attractive, effective and sustainable.

THE MEDIUM IS THE MESSAGE

THIS brings me to a larger question. Instead of starting an ethical business, would it be more effective to make as much money as possible by whatever legal means you can, and then to use it for good?

Bill Gates made his fortune by creating and exploiting a software monopoly. Chuck Feeney also created a monopoly and used it to sell alcohol and tobacco. A large portion of George Soros's wealth was earned on a single day – Black Wednesday, 16 September 1992 – when he shorted sterling and scooped over $1 billion.

Imagine how much greater their influence would have been – how much more good they would have done – if they had devoted their energy to running ethical businesses from day one. We are each on our own personal journey and I am certainly in no position to adopt a superior moral tone. But I believe that ethical businesses are, in and of themselves, a force for good.

CREATE YOUR OWN PERFECT WORLD

WHEN you launch a business, you have an opportunity to fashion your own perfect world. You control every aspect of it: what it will do, where it will be located, how it will behave, the principles by which it will be operated. Everything, in fact. Little wonder that some entrepreneurs demonstrate mildly megalomaniacal tendencies.

With Honey's we set out to create a company that reflected our beliefs and met our need for a certain type of dog food. There was as much dreaming as there was planning. When we thought of something we felt strongly about, we would work out how to incorporate it into the business. Here are a few examples of what I mean:

We hate call centres, the idea of monitoring calls, cubicle farms and telesales scripts.	Honey's customer care managers are able to work from home for part of the week, aren't monitored and, because they know their stuff, are free to speak from the heart.
We love companies where they give you the information you want and leave you to make your own mind up without sales pressure.	Honey's has no sales function and no sales staff.
We are suspicious of companies that talk about giving a percentage of profits to charity. This is meaningless because they can decide what to count as profit.	Honey's gives 1 per cent of sales to charity and then some.
We admire companies that admit it when they make a mistake, say sorry and try to put it right.	At Honey's we own up to mistakes immediately and then rush to try to put things right. Afterwards, we generally send a little 'sorry' gift. Plus, all customers have my personal email address in case they want to contact me about some aspect of our product or service they are unhappy about.

We had no idea whether what was important to us would prove to be important to others. We thought it would, but we didn't actually care because we were going to do it anyway.

HOW TO BUILD AN ETHICAL BUSINESS IN FIVE EASY STEPS

EVERY day we are faced with decisions that have ethical implications. Some of these decisions are relatively innocuous (using a work phone for personal calls), some complicated (telling a friend that they are being deceived by their spouse), and some deal with much larger concerns (buying clothes from fashion retailers that exploit workers in poorer countries).

To help us make these decisions we each have an inbuilt moral compass. This compass is what we use to differentiate between right and wrong and it determines how we are going to act in any given situation.

An organization is in exactly the same position. It, too, faces decisions that have ethical implications. Again, some of these decisions are relatively innocuous (paying someone a small amount of cash knowing that they may not declare it to the taxman), some complicated (using materials that aren't easily recycled), and some deal with much larger concerns (trading with companies in countries with a poor human rights record).

An organization also requires an inbuilt moral compass. This compass is what its employees will use to differentiate between right and wrong and it determines how they will act in any given situation.

Here are five simple steps you can follow to ensure that your company has an inbuilt moral compass that works.

Step one: Put it in writing

You don't need to write your own ethical beliefs down because they are integral to your very existence. Not so with a business, which is a separate entity. The principles on which a business is based and the way in which those principles are going to be applied must be obvious to its employees, suppliers and customers. The only way to achieve this is to write everything down in plain English.

This is how Recreational Equipment, Inc. (REI), an American company that makes and sells sporting goods, camping gear, travel equipment and clothes, summarizes its core values:

Being a consumer co-op, rather than a publicly traded company, enables us to focus on the long-term interests of the co-op and our members. We answer to you – our members – and run our business accordingly. It means that we're able to operate a business that plays a vital national role in growing outdoor participation and protecting the environment for future generations. Anyone may shop at REI, member or not. But co-op members pay $20 for a lifetime membership to join and receive a portion of the cooperative's profits each year based on a percentage of their eligible purchases, among many other benefits.

REI is a fascinating business. It was founded in 1938 and is the largest cooperative in America with

AN ORGANIZATION REQUIRES AN **INBUILT MORAL COMPASS** TO HELP ITS EMPLOYEES DIFFERENTIATE BETWEEN RIGHT AND WRONG...

...AND DETERMINE HOW THEY WILL ACT IN **ANY GIVEN SITUATION.**

a turnover of $2.5 billion, 12,000 employees and 143 shops.

Incidentally, I would advise you to give a wide berth to mission statements. You are running an ethical business not planning a military assault or a piece of espionage. Corporate mission statements are, almost without exception, vague, meaningless, boastful and pompous. Better to give your document a title such as: 'What We Believe in' or 'The Principles by Which We Run Our Business'.

What should go into your written document? It could cover:

- a description of the business's activities
- a description of the business's objectives
- the business's core beliefs and values
- the rules by which you will run the business
- how the business will treat staff
- how the business will treat customers
- how the business will treat suppliers
- how the business will care for the environment
- what the business will give back
- any goals the business may have and how performance will be monitored.

What you are creating is a sort of ethical manual. Keep it as short and concise as possible. Avoid jargon.

Step two: Make your expectations clear

You may be fortunate enough to have a team of people around you who subscribe to the same beliefs and values as you do and don't, therefore, require much in the way of guidance. Even so, it is important to make your expectations absolutely clear to both employees and suppliers. At Honey's we use a combination of one-to-one meetings, training sessions, videos, briefing sheets and booklets to ensure that our staff and producers understand what we expect and why.

Occasionally, a member of your team or a supplier will get something wrong. We discovered once that a newer member of Honey's staff hadn't fully taken on board that we offer unlimited free nutritional advice to anyone who asks and she had – basically – stopped answering questions from a particularly nervous member of the public. It was a genuine misunderstanding and the team member involved was mortified to have let us down.

It served as a reminder to us of the importance of training and led to a number of improvements.

On the other hand, when someone wilfully ignores your code of ethics, firm action is required. A few months after we started Honey's, we discovered that one of our butchers was supplying us with 'free-range chickens' that were, in fact, factory-farmed. We quickly dispensed with his services. We told those customers we believed had been affected and explained what measures we had put in place to make sure it didn't happen again. We offered a refund, too, although to the best of my knowledge no one accepted it.

There are times when it may be necessary to compromise. I once tried to talk Vicky into using humane rodent traps in the Honey's kitchens. Setting aside the problems associated with such traps (they must be checked every hour and the animals you catch must be released close to where the trap was set or they become disorientated and die) there wasn't anyone willing to handle the prisoners. We agreed instead on a policy of prevention (sealing every possible entry into the kitchens and using minimal amounts of poison). I wasn't entirely happy but I accepted that it was the best solution in the circumstances. Practical considerations sometimes trump principles.

YOU CAN'T EXPECT
YOUR EMPLOYEES,
SUPPLIERS AND
CUSTOMERS TO
ADHERE TO PRINCIPLES
YOU DON'T ADHERE
TO YOURSELF.

Step three: Lead from the front

There is no room for a 'do as I say, not as I do' approach when it comes to leading an ethical business. You can't expect your employees, suppliers and customers to adhere to principles you don't adhere to yourself.

Also, your ethical business will soon come unstuck if you don't involve all the stakeholders in the decision-making process. Ask everyone involved with your business for their ideas and input and provide them with feedback. By its very nature, an ethical business requires everyone's participation and support.

Another idea worth considering is doing away with all managers. One company that has achieved this is Morning Star, a tomato-canning business based in California. At Morning Star, nobody reports to a manager, because there are none. Instead, employees negotiate responsibilities with their peers and everyone can spend the company's money. Indeed, each individual is responsible for acquiring the tools needed to do his or her work. There are no titles and no promotions and compensation decisions are peer-based. Morning Star's goal is to create a company in which all team members: 'Will be self-managing professionals,

How to Build an Ethical Business...

initiating communications and the coordination of their activities with fellow colleagues, customers, suppliers, and fellow industry participants, absent directives from others.'

Everyone has to set their own personal mission (such as to turn tomatoes into tomato juice or to transport tomatoes from the field to the factory) and employees sign a Colleague Letter of Understanding with their peers in which they set out what they will be doing for the year ahead and what they will be paid. In most businesses, management salaries account for around 33 per cent of the total wage bill. Morning Star distributes most of what would otherwise go to managers back to its employees who are, as a result, paid well above the industry average. It is, by the way, one of the biggest tomato-canning businesses in the world with sales of over $700m a year.

Step four: Hire kind people

It is considerably easier to run an ethical business if you only employ people with the same passions, concerns and interests as yourself. This is relatively easy for small businesses (you don't need that many staff members) and urban businesses (plenty

63

of choice), but once you reach a certain size and/ or if you are in a rural location, it is much trickier.

To overcome this problem, the Honey's employment policy has always been to hire only people who are kind. We believe that if someone has a warm, caring and generous personality they will, as a matter of course, treat colleagues, customers and suppliers with proper respect.

After Honey's began to take off, we decided to try a DIY approach to solve our various recruitment needs. We placed advertisements on different online sites appealing for kind dog lovers to get in touch. There were about 500 replies and it took me the best part of two weeks to sift through all the CVs and send personal emails and letters to everyone who had contacted us. My responses often elicited further communications, all of which I answered.

Many companies no longer bother to acknowledge a job application, which is both short-sighted and rude. Anyway, we invited two groups of around twenty people each to a wine and cheese evening in a local restaurant. When they arrived, we gave them a name tag and took their photograph so that we could identify them afterwards. I gave a half-hour talk about the company and answered questions. Then Vicky and I circulated, making sure we spoke to everyone. After our guests had gone, we compared notes (using the photographs as reference) and asked the candidates who had most impressed us to a longer information session, which we paid them to attend (we also gave them a slap-up tea).

One of the most satisfying aspects of this early recruitment strategy was that many of the people we took on (and it is now eight years ago) are still with us. They (and others) have introduced friends and relatives also interested in working at Honey's HQ. Nowadays, Vicky operates a more formal interview approach, but we are still looking for the same core quality in an applicant: kindness.

As an aside, in order to attract kind and considerate employees you must, of course, show yourself to be a kind and considerate employer.

Step five: Monitor your ethical performance

Every business uses key indicators – such as sales, pending orders, debtors, wages, overheads and operating profits – to measure its performance. At Honey's we look at other indicators. How many books about canine nutrition did we sell or give

IT IS NOT ENOUGH
TO ANNOUNCE TO
THE WORLD THAT
YOU ARE A
**SOCIALLY
RESPONSIBLE
BUSINESS.**
YOU MUST HAVE
**HARD
EVIDENCE**
THAT YOU ARE.

away? How much did we donate to charity? How many farm visits did we undertake?

It is not enough to announce to the world that you are a socially responsible business. You must have hard evidence that you are. More than this, you must be able to demonstrate improvement in the areas that make you ethical.

You'll have to decide for yourself what is important to you, but the sort of areas you may want to consider include:

- environmental impact
- choice of suppliers
- employment policy
- wage policy
- not-for-profit activities
- campaigning
- charitable donations.

Within each of these categories there will be sub-categories. For example, when auditing your employment policy, you could include the number of employees with special needs you have working for you, or list the various ways in which your company is family-friendly. In each area, you need to establish a benchmark against which to monitor future improvements. At Honey's we waited until we were established for a few years before we benchmarked at all because it is easy to achieve improvements in the beginning, whereas once you are established you invariably have to try much, much harder.

TRYING TO DO THE BEST THING ISN'T ALWAYS STRAIGHTFORWARD

I am intolerant of companies that claim to be environmentally sustainable as it is virtually impossible to achieve. Humans are using up the world's resources faster than nature can replace them. According to the Global Footprint Network, in 2015 we consumed about 1.6 planets' worth of resources, and by 2030 that is expected to rise to two planets' worth. In fact, our greed has caused the planet's sixth extinction crisis. (The fifth extinction crisis, by the way, took place sixty-five million years ago with the loss of the dinosaurs.)

Species usually die off at a rate of around one to five a year. But at the moment we are losing species at 1,000 to 10,000 times the normal rate. Put another way, dozens of species are becoming extinct every day and within thirty years, between a third to a half of all species that existed when I was born are expected to have vanished. The primary cause is the rapidity with which we are driving habitat loss. Everything that lives on Planet Earth depends on intricate ecological webs. As ecosystems unravel, the extinction of one species is likely to lead to the loss of many, many more. The signs of imminent environmental disaster are everywhere. To offer just one example: we rely on bees to pollinate about a third of the crops we depend on for food, but bees, for reasons no one properly understands, are dying off in unprecedented numbers.

Governments are doing next to nothing to tackle the appalling damage humans are inflicting upon the environment. There is a lot of talk but negligible change. Businesses have, in many respects, much greater freedom to act. They aren't constrained by the need to please everyone or to win elections. They can, if they so wish, think long term. In a nutshell, having been part of the problem, businesses now have an opportunity to become part of the solution.

Of course, the size and complexity of the

environmental crisis facing us means that running even a relatively small environmentally sensitive company is far from easy. There are so many choices and so many decisions. Let me give you one real example.

Obviously, we have to put our dog food into some sort of container. These containers then have to be shipped to our customers. Naturally, we want to use as little packaging as possible and we would like it to be made from recycled materials and be recyclable. We also want to reduce the other resources required – freezer space, the type of transport and so forth.

After extensive experimentation and various trials, we found that the optimum way to package our food was in 'shires' – basically, thin, tubular, plastic sleeves that can be clipped at either end. We freeze these shires and then pack them into cardboard boxes with insulation sheets. The benefit of the shires is that they use a fraction of the material required by, say, a plastic tub. They weigh less, too, and once filled use up less space when stacked in a freezer. Because we do the freezing at Honey's HQ, we don't have to put freezer bags into the boxes and the insulation sheets are relatively slim. Nor do we have to pay for expensive, polluting, refrigerated transport.

Our packaging solution comes at a price. The only element that is made from partially recycled materials is the outer box (we tried 100 per cent recycled boxes but they disintegrated when wet). The plastic shires are not recyclable and it is difficult to recycle the insulation sheets and metal clips. Not a month passes without us considering other options. At one point, we tried to work a system that used rigid plastic cooler boxes, which would have been returned to us with every new order. Another time we flirted with wool insulation. We've considered second-hand cardboard boxes, too, and a sort of plastic pouch system.

Essentially, the current arrangement is what we believe to be the least bad option. There are hundreds of other areas within the business where similar decisions have to be made. What cleaning materials should we use? How do we cut back on our water usage? Can we completely eliminate food waste? Which utilizes less of the world's resources: an old, but well-maintained, freezer unit or something new and more efficient? I could, quite literally, go on and on and on. It is far from easy to reduce your carbon footprint even when you are trying hard.

The environment is not the only area we have to consider, either. We are frequently faced with ethical decisions. Fish offers dogs a great deal of nutrition and fresh fish scraps are relatively inexpensive. Should we offer fish recipes despite the fact that the fishing industry is destroying our oceans? Honey's Wiltshire HQ is closer to all of Ireland and most of France than it is to the north of Scotland. Given the trouble we sometimes have sourcing suitable ingredients within the UK, ought we to consider buying in from closer spots in Europe even though it would mean we could no longer boast that all our ingredients are British? Meat production is very un-environmental. Dogs are not obligate carnivores and can actually survive on a vegetarian and even vegan diet (I am going to talk more about this in a moment). Are we wrong to be in the raw-meat-and-bone dog food business in the first place?

'The whole problem with the world', according to Bertrand Russell, 'is that fools and fanatics are always so certain of themselves, but wiser people are full of doubts.' I don't feel in the least bit wise, but I am certainly full of doubts. By the by, Honey's doesn't sell dog food made with fish; we maintain our current policy of only buying British ingredients and we can, more or less, square our conscience with regard to being part of the meat industry.

Actually, I can't square my conscience about supporting the meat industry. Not a day passes without me thinking about ending my relationship with Honey's. I believe that killing any living creature is deeply wrong and I want no part in it. Like Macbeth, I feel: 'Will all great Neptune's ocean wash this blood clean from my hand?' Sooner or later I will end my involvement with the company, but I don't quite yet feel that I have achieved everything I would like.

More than anything else, I am hoping that by staying in the dog food business I will be in the best position to effect change. When I was much younger I was a great supporter of Greenpeace and PETA*-type activism. I didn't do anything especially dramatic but I went on demonstrations, signed petitions and donated what I could afford. I even stood outside factory gates and shouted through a megaphone. It made me feel less helpless but I am not sure how much I achieved.

So-called extreme behaviour is generally ignored by the people you are trying to influence. I have come to see that it can be just as valuable to be on the inside using less dramatic, more logical forms of persuasion. Honey's is putting increasing

---

* People for the Ethical Treatment of Animals

FOOLS AND
FANATICS
ARE ALWAYS SO
CERTAIN OF
THEMSELVES, BUT
**WISER
PEOPLE
ARE FULL
OF DOUBTS.**

pressure on other dog food manufacturers by proving that it is possible to give dogs a much healthier, more nutritious diet, show compassion to farm animals and *still* make money. Honey's is also winning hearts and minds amongst the dog-loving population. Dog-lovers, being animal-lovers, seem to me to be the consumers most likely to understand why humans need to stop eating meat.

There is another, more convoluted reason why I think that my years in dog food are not quite over. It follows from something John Berger says in his book *Why Look at Animals*. He points out that one of the major effects of industrialization is that humans in developed nations have almost no contact with other species. Our ancestors lived close to farm animals, used horses for transport and were much more likely to have daily encounters with wild animals and birds. Now zoo animals have become 'the living monument to their own disappearance'. If we hadn't domesticated the dog (and, in so far as they can be domesticated, the cat) many humans – the humans contributing most to the environmental calamity facing the world – would live in total isolation. Dogs serve to remind us that other species exist. They also have a positive effect on society, providing comfort and love and promoting responsibility and empathy.

If we are going to keep dogs then we owe it to them to give them a biologically appropriate diet. And a biologically appropriate diet for a dog is prey or its closest equivalent.

If you start an ethical business you, too, may find yourself thinking a great deal about bigger issues. You'll discover that trying to do the best thing isn't always straightforward.

HOW TO DEVELOP A WINNING IDEA

IF you have an urge to start an ethical business but haven't yet hit on the perfect idea, my advice would be to focus on a social wrong you would like to correct or a group of people you would like to help. Wherever there is injustice or human need there is, strangely enough, an ethical business opportunity.

• **Disgusted** by all the synthetic chemicals that make-up manufacturers put into their products? Start a natural make-up company.

• **Concerned** about food quality and the amount of packaging used by manufacturers and

supermarkets? Start an organic grocer that
sells everything by weight or volume and where
customers supply their own containers.

• **Keen to help** those living on the poverty line
in remote areas of, say, India? Start a fashion
house that trains women to produce accessories with the help of well-known Western
designers.

Many entrepreneurs feel that they need to
come up with a brand-new idea but it is often
better to take an existing concept and improve
it. The Plant Café is a chain of restaurants in
California that uses only seasonal, local, certified-
organic ingredients. They fit out their premises
with furniture made from recycled materials,
low-energy appliances and so forth. Their menu
is simple (it is the sort of place you would go for
breakfast or a sandwich and soup) and their prices
only slightly higher than equivalent offerings.
There is nothing especially unusual about The
Plant Café apart from the company's commitment
to sustainability. All the owners have done is
apply their ethical beliefs to a very straightforward
business.

One of the considerations when planning any business is scalability. Does your concept offer potential for major growth and how difficult will that growth be to achieve? Honey's has not proved readily scalable because high-quality ingredients at a cost-effective price are difficult to obtain, it takes a long time to train staff so that they are competent to talk to our customers about canine health and nutrition, and our food is noticeably more expensive than a mass-produced alternative.

Ethical businesses can be harder to scale because so much more thought and effort has to be put into every aspect of their operation. Still, there are plenty of businesses that have achieved it. Interface, the world's largest manufacturer of modular carpet systems (carpet tiles to you and me), for example, has one of the best sustainability records in the world. In 1994, the company's founder, Ray C. Anderson, read *The Ecology of Commerce*, in which the author, Paul Hawken, argues that the industrial system is destroying our planet and only industry leaders are powerful enough to stop it. As a result, Interface changed its whole approach to business, announcing that:

We will honour the places where we do business by endeavouring to become the first name in industrial ecology, a corporation that cherishes nature and restores the environment. Interface will lead by example and validate by results, including profits, leaving the world a better place than when we began, and we will be restorative through the power of our influence in the world.

In a highly competitive, price-sensitive market it is interesting to note that Interface not only transformed its environmental record but also managed huge growth and increased profitability.

Anderson already owned Interface when he had his epiphany. He took an existing business and completely altered everything about it. So dramatic was the change in approach that it was almost as if the company had been acquired by new owners. This leads on to another question that many entrepreneurs ask themselves: make or buy? Is it better to start a new business from scratch or to purchase an existing business and improve it?

The received opinion is that it is better to make than to buy because you can shape it exactly as you wish and lower levels of investment are required. I don't entirely agree. There are times when it is more sensible to buy a business and refashion it. I believe that in the future the market for environmentally friendly building supplies is

WHEREVER THERE
IS INJUSTICE OR
**HUMAN
NEED**
THERE IS,
STRANGELY
ENOUGH, AN
ETHICAL
BUSINESS
OPPORTUNITY.

going to expand dramatically. This is partly for ecological reasons and partly because many of the processes and chemicals used in the manufacture of building materials have associated human health risks. I have no desire to enter this sector but if I did, I think I would be tempted to take over an existing retailer and change its focus. This would give me instant access to premises, stock, cash flow, expert staff, suppliers and customers. I could be turning the business into what I wanted it to be in a matter of weeks rather than spending years building it from scratch. It is a fallacy that all ethical businesses have to be new businesses.

THERE IS A SIMPLE, INEXPENSIVE WAY TO TEST YOUR BUSINESS IDEA

ETHICAL businesses do not succeed simply because they are ethical. They must be based on a commercially viable idea. How can you assess whether the idea is any good? You could do what big companies do: invite groups of prospective customers into a room and cross-examine them. This approach is not without merit but there are better ways, in my opinion, of gauging what demand will be like.

For small, relatively inexpensive products you could create samples and try to sell them. According to its website (*innocentdrinks.co.uk/us/*

our-story), this is how Innocent, the ethical drinks company, was launched:

> We started Innocent in 1999 after selling our smoothies at a music festival. We put up a big sign asking people if they thought we should give up our jobs to make smoothies, and put a bin saying 'Yes' and a bin saying 'No' in front of the stall. Then we got people to vote with their empties. At the end of the weekend, the 'Yes' bin was full, so we resigned from our jobs the next day and got cracking.

If what you want to do is too complicated or expensive actually to create, then try an 'as if' test. So, for example, if you're thinking of starting an environmentally sensitive office and domestic cleaning service using only plant-based products and water, run a small marketing campaign (advertisements, phone calls and mail shots) *as if* it actually existed and – from the response – you will have a good feel for likely interest. You can use this approach, incidentally, for surprisingly big projects. I've seen it done by everyone from book publishers to property developers. This way of putting one's toe in the water is referred to as 'dry testing' – a bit like a dry run.

Ethical
BUSINESSES
DO NOT SUCCEED
SIMPLY BECAUSE THEY
ARE ETHICAL. THEY MUST
BE BASED ON A
commercially
viable
IDEA.

Another brilliant way to gauge your idea's potential is to seek crowdfunding from an online community such as Kickstarter or Indiegogo. I am going to talk about raising money from crowdfunding sites separately. At this juncture, I just want to point out that they offer a fantastic, virtually zero-cost way of finding out if your new business concept has legs.

TELL YOUR STORY

IN 2001, Tom Szaky, a student at Princeton, noticed that some of his friends were achieving much higher yields from their marijuana plants by growing them in compost created with the help of worms. He and his friend, Jon Beyer, began to read about vermiculture and ran experiments in their college dormitories. They found that by introducing worms to organic waste they could create two products: potting soil and liquid plant food. Certain that there would be a market for a completely natural, 100 per cent safe, really effective fertilizer, they managed to persuade friends and relatives to lend them $20,000, with which they bought a continuous-flow composting system and some worms. Their raw ingredient

– waste – was donated free of charge by their college. Unable to afford new packaging, they bought old plastic drinks bottles collected on their behalf by churches and schools, which they then washed out by hand. The company they started, TerraCycle, has become one of the most innovative recycling businesses in the world. It specializes in taking every conceivable type of consumer waste and turning it into useful products. To give you a feel for its size, TerraCycle acquires waste material from some sixty-five million collectors in twenty countries and makes sufficient profits to have donated over $15 million to charity. One of the reasons for its success is that the business is based on a great story.

From earliest times stories have played an important role in human communication. They not only entertain, but also educate, inform, amuse, warn, remind and comfort us. It is no coincidence that every religious and political leader down through history has employed storytelling as a means of persuasion. Nor is it a coincidence that the most successful businesses employ the same techniques. A convincing story can capture hearts, minds and wallets.

This book is all about the Honey's story and you'll notice that it is actually made up of a lot of smaller stories, each of which illustrates a different principle on which the business is based. In my experience, people tend to be turned off by a barrage of facts. This is why, when I am explaining what Honey's does to customers, potential customers, suppliers, colleagues, veterinary professionals, journalists or anyone else, I try to make it more interesting and more memorable through the use of stories.

To offer just one example, when I want to discuss how wicked and exploitative processed dog food manufacturers are, I tend to begin with the history of dog food. I open with a 2,000-year-old quote from the Roman poet Juvenal: *Et farris sordes mordere canini* – 'And he bit into in the filth of a dog's bread'. Then I talk about how James Spratt, the nineteenth-century American founder of modern dog food, was inspired to use waste ingredients after watching dogs eat old ships' tack on the Liverpool docks and mention how an oversupply of horses after the First World War led to a product called Ken-L Ration, which was made from horsemeat.

Think of your business in terms of different stories. Throw your net wide: how you came up with the idea, the market you are operating in, your early struggles, your customers' experiences,

THE MOST SUCCESSFUL BUSINESSES USE STORYTELLING AS A MEANS OF PERSUASION.

A CONVINCING STORY CAN CAPTURE HEARTS, MINDS AND WALLETS.

the history of whatever you are doing, and anything else that makes your business come alive. Keep your stories human and – where relevant – don't be afraid of employing different emotions such as humour, fear and pity. Emotion forges connections. Remember, too, that a story can be told face-to-face, over the phone, in print, via a podcast, via a video, and in a hundred other ways. For example, when I posted a video on our Facebook page entitled *The unpalatable truth about dog food* over 10,000 people looked at it in the first three days.

WHY I LIKE BUSINESSES WITH LOTS OF SMALL CUSTOMERS

MY first proper business was an advertising agency that specialized in direct response – that is any marketing communication that produces a measurable result, such as an advertisement with a coupon, a television commercial with a phone number or what is generally referred to as junk mail. The agency grew to be a reasonable size and had a blue-chip client list that included companies such as American Express, the *Financial Times* and Marks & Spencer. I hated the work (which was boring) and the industry (which was amoral). Most of all, I hated our clients. A few of them were decent enough and one or two (such as Vicky) ended up becoming real friends. By and large, however, the sort of people who seek employment in the marketing departments of large companies are unreasonable, demanding, narcissistic and not terribly bright. I spent almost all my time sucking up to them and pandering to their various whims and fancies. I was annoyed by the fact that no matter how good we were, there was always the risk that a client would suddenly fire us. When I sold the agency, I decided that never again would I run a business reliant on a small number of customers, each spending a large amount of money. Honey's has several thousand customers, and although it breaks my heart when we lose one (and, thank heavens, it is rare enough), it doesn't affect the business as a whole.

After I sold my advertising agency, I was under the misapprehension that I was a businessman, whereas, in fact, I was just a copywriter who had got lucky. Anyway, I invested in around a dozen small businesses. Three – an art dealership, a chauffeur-driven car service and a shampoo manufacturer – received all their sales through wholesalers, agents or retailers to whom they paid commission. I resented the reduced income. It worried me that the businesses I had invested in were dependent on others to sell our goods and services. I didn't like the fact that my businesses had no relationship with the actual customers. I didn't make any money as a business angel but I did learn a great deal. In particular, I realized that if I ever became involved with a business again, I wanted it to have a direct relationship with the end user. This is the main reason why Honey's doesn't sell its food through third parties. (Another is that we haven't the margin.)

It is up to you to decide on a business model that will suit both you and your enterprise. As I have explained, I prefer businesses with lots of customers who order direct. The key advantages of this are:

- You don't have to worry about losing individual customers.
- You aren't reliant on anyone else.
- You can keep all (or virtually all) of the income.
- You own the relationship with the customer, which will open up all sorts of other benefits and opportunities.

There are other aspects of Honey's business model that I would recommend. I have already mentioned the lack of a sales function. We find that prospective customers really appreciate that we never, ever try to sell them anything. As it happens, it is not in our interest because we lose a substantial sum of money on all new orders owing to our very narrow margins and large set-up costs (a first-order discount, an average of an hour on the telephone discussing the dog's needs, a free book, follow-up calls, etc.). Indeed, we estimate that it takes us around five months to break even on a new customer. Our business model is, therefore, to make a small amount of profit from our customers every month over a very long period of time. These customers are under no obligation to order so we must provide them with first-class food, service and value for money or we will be out of pocket. In plain English, if we talk someone into buying from us and they only place one order because Honey's isn't really for them, we are wasting our time and money.

Part of our 'absolutely no sales pressure, build a genuine relationship with the customer' approach is that we don't offer online ordering. We believe that if you have to call and speak to us then you must be serious about raw feeding *plus* it offers us an opportunity to really get to know you (and for you to get to know us). Recently, a number of existing customers have asked if we would introduce online ordering and Vicky is really keen on it, too. So, although it was not part of our original business model, by the time this book has been printed there may be a shop for returning customers on our website. It is important to remain flexible.

WHAT TO INCLUDE IN AN ETHICAL BUSINESS PLAN

BUSINESS plans tend to follow an identical formula. They begin with an executive summary and then plod through the commercial potential, how it can be exploited, why the founders are the best people to exploit it, the money that could be made from the proposed exploitation, and how much funding is required to carry out the exploitation. They put forward best-case and worst-case scenarios and analyse strengths and weaknesses, opportunities and threats. They are, by their very nature, wildly optimistic documents and, as an aside, all of them, without exception, describe the one scenario that will never, ever occur. This is because, as Helmuth von Moltke the Elder so succinctly put it: 'No battle plan survives contact with the enemy.'

Ethical business plans are an altogether different proposition. They certainly can include market analysis and the founders' résumés, spreadsheets and exit strategies, but their core element is always going to be the enterprise's non-commercial objectives. What is needed is a document that discusses the wider issues and explains why you are starting the business, what you hope to achieve and how you hope to achieve it.

You may like to utilize an accounting principle that is often referred to as the 'triple bottom line'. The term was first used by John Elkington in his book *Cannibals with Forks: The Triple Bottom Line of 21st Century Business*. In it he argues that companies should be preparing three different (and quite separate) bottom lines:

- The bottom line of the profit and loss account.

- The bottom line of a company's 'people account' – a measure of how socially responsible an organization is.

- The bottom line of a company's 'planet' account – a measure of how environmentally responsible it has been.

BUSINESS PLANS ARE **WILDLY OPTIMISTIC** DOCUMENTS AND DESCRIBE THE ONE SCENARIO THAT WILL NEVER, EVER OCCUR.

The *Economist* summarized this neatly:

The triple bottom line (TBL) thus consists of three Ps: profit, people and planet. It aims to measure the financial, social and environmental performance of the corporation over a period of time. Only a company that produces a TBL is taking account of the full cost involved in doing business.

Incidentally, the title of Elkington's book is a reference to a question posed by the Polish poet Stanislaw Lec: 'Is it progress if a cannibal uses a fork?' So, although Elkington proposes that corporations should be held accountable to the 'triple bottom line' of economic prosperity, environmental quality and social justice, at the same time he questions whether doing so actually constitutes progress.

As Honey's was funded by three people (Vicky, my best friend and me), we never bothered with a formal business plan. It didn't require much cash and we *could* afford to lose our money, so we just got on with it. However, right at the beginning, I did write a long, long essay covering: canine anatomy, canine nutrition, why dogs should be fed raw food, the raw feeding movement, the history of dog food, how dog food manufacturers are ruining our dogs' health and shortening their lives, and everything that is wrong with the British agri-food sector (starting with a condemnation of farming practices and ending with an attack on supermarket chains). We used that essay as the basis of the briefs we prepared for staff, suppliers and customers. We posted it on our website and eventually I turned it into *Honey's Natural Feeding Handbook for Dogs* (available in all good bookshops!).

Before all that, however, it served as a blueprint for the enterprise and we referred to it regularly during the planning process. Even if you don't need a detailed document, I really recommend putting the principles by which you intend to run your business down in writing.

GIVE BECAUSE IT IS GOOD TO GIVE, NOT JUST BECAUSE IT IS GOOD FOR BUSINESS

'NO one', as Anne Frank pointed out, 'has ever become poor by giving.' If I have learnt one thing from all my years in business, it is to give. I am not talking about the painless, tax-deductible donations most businesses make to charity, or the other acts of apparent generosity such as paying slightly above-average wages or offering work experience to young people or sponsoring local sports clubs. I am talking about making the act of giving the core of your whole enterprise and giving things away that you can't always afford to part with. Ralph Waldo Emerson put it well: 'The only gift is a portion of thyself.'

You could give your business's money, of course, and this is well worth doing. But you could also give your business's time, knowledge, resources, expertise and even its love. There is plenty of evidence that humans benefit from giving, including:

- A **Harvard Business School** study that showed how giving money to someone else lifted participants' happiness more than spending it on themselves.

- A similar study by the **University of California**, Riverside, in which participants performed five acts of kindness each week for six weeks, also lifted participants' happiness.

- A **National Institutes of Health** research programme, which found that when people give to charities, it activates regions of the brain associated with pleasure, social connection and trust.

- **Scientific research**, which has shown that altruistic behaviour releases endorphins in the brain. In addition, it releases oxytocin, another hormone (also released during sex and breast-feeding) that induces feelings of warmth, euphoria and connection to others.

• A study by the **University of California**, Berkeley, which found that elderly volunteers with the identical health profile were 44 per cent less likely to die over a five-year period than non-volunteers.

• A **University of California** study, this time in San Diego, which proved that when one person behaves generously it inspires observers to behave generously later, towards different people.

As with so much else in life, what holds true for individuals, holds true for organizations. Genuinely altruistic organizations see innumerable benefits. I know this from first-hand experience. The more Honey's gives away, the better we feel about ourselves, the more people (employees, suppliers and customers) want to become involved with us. We have no formal giving policy but it is integral to the way we operate. It would be impossible to list all the different ways it manifests itself, but I can offer a few examples:

- We will show anyone **how to make the same food** that we sell. We'll give them recipes, we'll offer them advice and we'll support them through the whole process. We'll even tell them how to buy the ingredients at the lowest possible price.

- We will provide **unlimited, free access to our Health Team** by telephone and email. This team includes vets, veterinary nurses and nutritionists and is headed up by an escapee from the pharmaceutical sector. Together they probably represent the single largest raw-feeding resource in Europe.

- We will give **free copies of our books** and other literature to anyone who asks. We also give them away to not-for-profit organizations to sell as fundraisers.

- We give **advice and expertise** to other entre-preneurs and businesses that are interested in raw feeding. If we think they are serious (and share our ethical values) we'll offer them a tour of our kitchens and help them get started.

- We never turn away any good **animal-related**

cause that approaches us. We give them cash, free food, hampers to raffle, fundraising advice, free printing, free use of our video-making facilities – anything, in fact, that seems appropriate or helpful.

• Every time we sell a packet of our ethical dog treats, Beautiful Joe's – more of which later – we **donate** the same volume to a **rescue centre**.

• We become **involved with our customers**. We sometimes perform services that have nothing to do with making dog food, such as a rehoming a dog or introducing customers with common interests to each other.

This is before our larger cash donations, our public research programme, the free food we give to customers who are having temporary financial problems and a host of other activities.

Although we mention aspects of our giving policy on our website and elsewhere, we try not to make too much of a fuss about it. The good is taken out of giving when the donor is doing it for reasons of self-gratification. Giving should be as anonymous as possible.

GOOD MONEY

I feel that the American Quaker missionary
Stephen Grellet got it right when he said:

> I expect to pass through life but once. If there-
> fore, there be any kindness I can show, or any
> good thing I can do to any fellow being, let me do
> it now, and not defer or neglect it, as I shall not
> pass this way again.

MAKE YOUR MISTAKES WHEN YOU ARE SMALL

ON 30 March 2011, Vicky sent the following (personalized) letter to each and every Honey's customer:

> The reason I am writing is because we have had a bit of a – well – Swedish problem. In our enthusiasm to use only fresh, local, seasonal vegetables, about a month ago we decided to include swede from a farm just over the road in some of our recipes.
>
> The thing about swede is that it has a strong smell and flavour and although most of our canine customers have been fine with it, a few have said to us (in dog language, of course):

'It may be good for me, but I still don't like it.' Hopefully, you won't have encountered this problem, but if you have (and we don't yet know about it) please get in touch so that we can put things right for you. We'll happily replace any food you are unhappy about or give you a full refund plus a little 'so sorry' gift to make up for the inconvenience.

We won't, I hasten to add, be using swede again!

Swedegate, as the incident came to be known internally, cost the company around £15,000 at a time when the loss of £15,000 really hurt. As far as we could make out, the problem was a result of super-fresh swede and beef juices mingling inside each packet. It was certainly an explosive mix because in certain instances it caused the plastic to blow out. Most customers, once reassured that there were no food safety implications, held their noses and served it up. Most dogs seemed to relish the foul smell and a few customers actually asked if we would make the recipe again. We replaced £10,800 worth of food and spent £3–4,000 on gifts and thank-you cards to all our victims. Only two customers asked to be refunded, and both reordered a month later.

OWN UP TO YOUR MISTAKES, SHOW YOUR CUSTOMERS YOU CARE AND DO YOUR BEST TO **PUT THINGS RIGHT** (WHATEVER THE FINANCIAL COST).

When Swedegate occurred, we only had a few hundred customers. We called each of them several times as the disaster unfolded. Initially, to say that there might be a problem, then, when we had worked out what had happened, to explain the cause and arrange replacement food, and finally to apologize again and to have a general chat. Later on, we sent individual, proper, old-fashioned letters of apology. Interestingly, sales shot up that spring. We learnt quite a bit from the experience, viz. own up to your mistakes, show your customers you care and do your best to put things right whatever the financial cost. We also learnt that it is less bothersome and considerably cheaper to make your mistakes when you are small. The same mistake today would cost us four or five times as much and we'd have to bring in extra staff to make the calls.

THE LAST THING YOU NEED IS MONEY

IT is much better to launch a business on a shoestring. This is because businesses that begin life with too much cash get into bad habits. They waste money and build bureaucracy. Also, any concept that requires a great deal of capital in order to get off the ground is, basically, untested. Untold numbers of businesses fail simply because their founders were determined to run before they could walk.

Hard-up entrepreneurs are forced to be more creative. They don't have cash to throw at a problem, so they solve it by other means. Being under-resourced, they are forced from day one to have lots of contact with their customers. This in turn means that they build invaluable experience about what will and won't work.

When Vicky and I were planning to manufacture a new type of dog food, we couldn't find anyone to advise us on how to make it. For several months, we travelled all over the country looking at complicated bits of equipment and wondering whether we could adapt them to our requirements. The equipment manufacturers we talked to were very patient and helpful. It must have been a nuisance to them to have two people with no practical experience asking them what were sometimes, in hindsight, rather stupid questions. While we were looking for the equipment, Vicky experimented at home with different recipes using locally sourced meat and vegetables. This, the first stage of development, cost us almost nothing – some petrol and some ingredients.

It was clear that if we were going to set up a new commercial kitchen we would need to invest a substantial sum of money. We had the money and we weren't worried about losing it. However, we hadn't worked the production process out and we knew nothing about this type of manufacturing. We didn't want to buy equipment that could turn out to be unsuitable. Instead, Vicky visited various local butchers until she found one willing to make the food for us. He quoted a price per 250g and 500g packet of food and we just added on our profit margin when selling it to customers. This, the first stage of development, cost us just an advance on account for the butcher. It was only later, when the business was up and running and profitable, that we set up our own commercial kitchen and took over the means of production. In the early days, we didn't even have an office, but ran everything from Vicky's home.

Incidentally, establishing our own commercial kitchen did not require a great deal of capital. The premises we moved into had been untenanted for several years and the landlord was happy for us to have it rent-free provided we paid the business rates. As the previous tenants had been operating a smokehouse, it came complete with fridges and freezers that we were able to get working – another huge saving. The equipment we purchased was all second-hand and the dealer offered us a twelve-month private finance deal.

Based on mine and Vicky's experiences of setting up Honey's, here are five lessons I have learnt for how to keep new business investment requirements to a bare minimum:

• **Don't hang about**. The sooner you start selling your product or service, the sooner you'll have income coming in. Don't wait until everything is perfect. If you haven't got the money to go into production, create an acceptable prototype and sell from that.

• **Keep your day job**. If you can't afford to give up paid employment then start your new business in the evenings and at weekends. Remember, you are your own best employee. If you can save money by doing a job yourself, do it. There is another advantage to this. It sends a strong message out to your customers, suppliers and employees that you aren't afraid to roll up your sleeves and that you understand the value of money.

• **Get family and friends involved**. Don't hesitate to ask others for help.

• **Don't waste a penny**. Run your business from the cheapest possible premises (perhaps your home), buy good second-hand equipment, borrow and barter where you can. Make do. Lots of expenditure that seems necessary can often be avoided.

- **Fail quickly**. Some business ideas need refining and more time. Others are turkeys and it's a good idea to discover this quickly. Obviously, you don't want to give up too soon, but equally, there can be a disproportionately high cost to carrying on when it is clear that your concept is not a winner.

The thing about an ethical business is that almost everyone – customers, suppliers and employees – is likely to share your values. They will be keen to support you and will understand why you are economizing wherever you can. Naturally, they expect socially responsible businesses to avoid waste and to live up to the principle of 'reduce, recycle, reuse'.

WHY YOU SHOULD AVOID OUTSIDE FUNDING

VICKY and I found what money we needed to get Honey's up and running from our own resources. Later, my best friend lent us some cash to fund some of the non-essential projects we were keen to undertake – such as publishing a book and taking a stand at Crufts.

Funding Honey's ourselves gave us a massive advantage. We had no one else to please – apart, of course, from our customers. It allowed us to hold true to our beliefs, too. Honey's spends money on all sorts of activities that an outside investor, keen to reduce costs and optimize returns, might not understand or approve of.

If you need more money than you can raise

from your own resources, family and friends – and you can't persuade your suppliers or prospective customers to support you – then your first port of call should almost certainly be one of the crowdfunding sites. Crowdfunding can be used to find investors or to pre-sell your service or product. It offers a fast and inexpensive way to reach investors and customers. What's more, you can select a platform that attracts socially responsible and aware visitors who are likely to understand and share your goals. Best of all, crowdfunding allows you to test your concept prior to launching it.

If you need more cash than you can easily raise to fund your business idea, my advice is to drop it and come up with something else. Starting a business is a gamble. If you only play with money you really can afford to lose, it takes all the pressure off.

SUFFER SOME LOSSES AND AVOID THE LAW

ONE of the reasons why ethical businesses may outperform purely profit-driven enterprises is that they are, by their very nature, more open and trusting. There can, however, be a price to pay for believing the best of others and taking people at face value; I often feel that Honey's suffers disproportionately more than other businesses in this respect. A research consultant we employed for three years turned out to have delivered results that can best be described as dubious, and we had to start the project all over again; a computer supplier talked us into a ludicrously expensive IT system that never worked and, with hindsight, never could have worked; and an equipment manufacturer to whom we paid a sizeable sum failed to deliver equipment that was fit for purpose and refused to put it right or make a refund.

Since we started our business we have, therefore, suffered repeated and sometimes fairly heavy losses. While some of these losses are, without doubt, down to our gullibility, the majority can be attributed to the fact that Vicky and I have an unshakable belief in the honesty and integrity of others. Naturally, it is annoying when we find out that we have made an error of judgement, but there is little point in upbraiding either ourselves or the other party. We have no intention of changing our philosophy. There is no place, in our opinion, for the cynical or suspicious in a not-only-for-profit enterprise. Anyway, whenever we come to consider the people who have fooled us, we have found that they are more to be pitied than censured.

I am not, I hasten to add, proposing that socially responsible entrepreneurs can afford to throw all caution to the wind. One must observe normal, prudent business practice. Still, to my mind, if you want to enjoy the benefits that flow from establishing a truly ethical business, you must accept that they will open you to being taken advantage of.

Our approach to what a more cautious business might consider to be avoidable losses is matched by

IF YOU WANT
TO ENJOY
**THE
BENEFITS
THAT FLOW**
FROM ESTABLISHING
A TRULY
**ETHICAL
BUSINESS**
YOU MUST ACCEPT
THAT THEY WILL
OPEN YOU TO
BEING TAKEN
ADVANTAGE OF.

an unwillingness to litigate. Never say never, but to date we have not sued anyone who has stolen from us or caused us to lose money. However, we are obsessive note-takers, report-writers and email-senders – frankly, we document everything, no matter how trivial. So, if we were of a mind to pursue someone through the courts we would certainly have the evidence to back up our case. What puts us off isn't so much the cost or the time (although these are considerations), but the fact that litigation is, essentially, negative. Better, we feel, to focus our energies on something positive. Anyway, winning a court case is a pyrrhic victory. Perhaps you will get back the money you have lost and possibly, if you are super lucky, your legal expenses. Very, very rarely you'll be given some compensation. But it is a depressing and dispiriting thing to be constantly reliving old injustices.

Our unwillingness to enter into litigation has had some unusual side effects. For instance, our company owns the trademark to the name 'Honey's' in relation to dog treats, dog food and so forth. For several years, another company has been infring-ing this trademark and despite polite requests has refused to change its name. The law is clear on this issue and we could certainly force them to stop and expect to receive compensation for our losses.

We reason, though, that their behaviour doesn't cost us *that* much business and we dislike the idea of behaving in an aggressive way to anyone, no matter how justified.

Our lack of enthusiasm for litigation is why we don't bother with solicitors or contracts. Apart from employment contracts (which are designed to protect our employees more than the company), we don't go in for much in the way of legal documents. Our terms and conditions were copied and pasted from another company. If we enter into an agreement with a third party we generally just send a memo about it or, if we are in a grown-up mood, a letter setting out the nature of the agreement. This has the added advantage of saving us a great deal of bother and money. According to the *Law Society Gazette*, small- to medium-sized businesses in the UK spend a staggering £9 billion a year on legal services. We see no point in contributing to this figure.

DON'T WORRY ABOUT THE COMPETITION

'THE man who can keep a secret may be wise,' according to the American author E. W. Howe, 'but he is not half as wise as the man who has no secrets to keep.' Whether you are involved with a microbusiness or a multinational there are no benefits (and plenty of drawbacks) to keeping your business plans secret.

The argument advanced against total transparency is that competitors will steal your ideas. The truth is that this is very unlikely. The number of individuals and organizations in a position to be able to benefit from something you have thought up is going to be extremely small. Anyway, suppose you do manage to bring a new product or service

**NOTHING BUILDS
TRUST LIKE
OPENNESS.**

to market without your competitors hearing of it. The moment you start the sales process anyone who is so minded will be able to copy it. Suppose you develop some new technique or system or marketing approach? Again, sooner or later others are going to learn of it.

The fact is, if a competitor is smart enough to take your concept and use it to their advantage they would almost certainly flourish with or without you. In my experience, as it happens, there is a much greater chance that a competitor will take an idea and make a hash of it. Bluntly, in over four decades of being in business, including a decade spent running a large advertising agency and dealing with hundreds of other businesses, I can't recall a single occasion when there has been any purpose whatsoever to keeping an idea secret. All that an obsession with confidentiality does is waste valuable time and energy, which could be put to better use.

What are the arguments in favour of total transparency? One of the biggest assets any business can have is its stakeholders' trust. Nothing builds trust like openness. Honey's publishes its recipes, research, new product ideas and other business plans. We have always answered with complete candour any question put to us. I can't think, offhand, of any information to do with the current or future operation of the company that we wouldn't be happy to share. Our sincerity and directness gives customers, staff and suppliers confidence in us. We are happy if we can help someone else, including other businesses.

Another point. Things move quickly in business. If you want to stay ahead, you have to innovate. If you don't, sooner or later you will fail. On this basis, it doesn't really matter if other businesses copy you. You will always be one step ahead.

AVOID POINTLESS FIGHTS

I may be averse to litigation but that doesn't mean I don't sometimes yearn for a fight. Honey's is, so far as I know, the only British company that makes dog food using ingredients that are 100 per cent suitable for human consumption in a kitchen that meets all the hygiene standards required for the preparation of human food. For the first few years of business we were regulated by our local Trading Standards office. However, at a certain point someone – I have always suspected a jealous competitor – pointed out that we ought to be regulated and inspected by the Department for Environment, Food and Rural Affairs (Defra), which is responsible for the animal feed industry.

Because highly processed, manufactured dog food is made, almost without exception, using animal by-products and derivatives of the lowest possible quality (often including rotten meat), Defra's predominant concern is to avoid cross-contamination. Furthermore, their operating rules were not written with the production of raw dog food in mind and so are unclear to the point of being contradictory on the subject. From a safe distance – I was living in America at the time – I pressed Vicky to tell the local Defra team to go boil their heads and to insist we should continue to be audited by Trading Standards and no one else.

This was not the first time I had urged Vicky to defy authority. Another example related to our name. Honey's Real Dog Food actually started life as Darling's Real Dog Food. It came to our attention, however, that the trademark for the name 'Darling' belonged to Nestlé. As Nestlé only seemed to be marketing tiny amounts of Darling Dog Food in Estonia (or possibly Latvia, it is a long time ago) it seemed to me that we could afford to defy them.

In these (and various other) instances I saw our company as a David tackling a Goliath. Even if we lost I felt that we would attract lots of publicity and sympathy. Vicky always sticks to the same line whenever I start spoiling for a dust-up: we can't afford to be diverted from the main matter in hand – spreading the word about species-appropriate nutrition, campaigning for better farm animal welfare and surviving. Her motto is that we should avoid pointless fights. She is right. Which is why we are now Honey's and not Darling's.

GET OUT THERE

ON Wednesday, 17 February 2010, I travelled by plane, train and automobile from Ireland to a place called Death Hill in Durham where I addressed a small group of dog-lovers interested in learning about raw feeding. It was one of hundreds of such talks that Vicky, Ruth (now head of our Health Team), Katie (our research manager) and, to a lesser extent, I have given over the years to dog clubs, vets, veterinary nurses, students, dog behaviourists and other canine professionals. Giving such talks is surprisingly expensive when you add up the cost of transport, salaries (where relevant) and accommodation, not to mention the food and literature we always give away. I remember the Death Hill talk in particular because it was a foul night, only half a dozen people turned up and at the end of the evening, when I asked if any of them were now tempted to try raw feeding, they all said, without hesitation, that they weren't.

Even a really successful seminar will only result in half a dozen trial offers. No event that we have ever been involved with has ever come close to paying for itself. Yet, we still accept a high percentage of the invitations we receive. Why do we do this? Because we have actually met and spent time with them, the few customers we do win this way frequently become friends and generally stay with us indefinitely. More significantly, there isn't a better way of finding out what is and isn't important to our customers and prospective customers.

If you aren't in a business that lends itself to giving talks or attending events, there are plenty of other ways of meeting possible customers. Leo Burnett, the famous American advertising guru, was in the habit of visiting potential clients' offices and waiting in reception until they agreed to see him (it is difficult to say 'no' to someone who has travelled halfway across the country on the off-chance of an audience). When my own advertising agency started working for NatWest Bank in the 1980s, I adapted Burnett's strategy. Without telling anyone in its head office, I made several trips to NatWest branches in distant parts of the UK, dropping in on them unannounced and introducing myself to the managers. Before long, word got back to NatWest's marketing director, who was so impressed with my enthusiasm that he gave my company considerably more work.

If you want to build a strong business, my advice is to get out there and meet people.

BE CAREFUL WHO YOU GIVE SHARES TO

THERE is a great temptation when you start a business to give shares to people who have been helping and supporting you. I did this with my first advertising agency – scattering shares like confetti on the staff. When the business was being acquired by a much bigger agency, one of my shareholding employees refused to sell his shares for the same price as everyone else. There were various legal options open to me that would have forced him to comply but they would have all taken time and cost money. Instead, I gave him the extra cash he demanded. I was annoyed, but what comes around, goes around. Anyway, there are lots of creative ways in which you can reward your employees that don't require you to give up equity.

BE AN EXPERT, NOT JUST AN ENTREPRENEUR

ETHICAL businesses are, by their very nature, going to be involved with bigger issues than simply providing products and/or services.

Vicky and I describe ourselves as artisan dog food producers but in truth the manufacturing process is pretty straightforward. If we have any expertise (and the more we learn, the more we realize how ignorant we are), it is in a whole host of related areas such as canine nutrition, canine health, animal rights, the agri-food sector and protecting the environment. I have attended the dissection of a grey wolf while Vicky has spent untold hours studying plastic recycling processes. I have interviewed professors of biology and Vicky

ETHICAL BUSINESSES CAN GAIN A **VERY REAL ADVANTAGE** BY WIDENING THEIR STUDY AND RESEARCH PROGRAMMES TO INCLUDE TOPICS THAT ARE NOT DIRECTLY RELATED TO THEIR DAY-TO-DAY ACTIVITIES.

has run extensive trials with obese dogs. Our growing knowledge base (and that of our colleagues) is what makes us stand out in our particular sector. It is why we are quoted in the media and invited to speak at professional conferences and asked to sit on industry bodies such as the Pet Food Manufacturers Association (PFMA).

When most businesses invest in training and education it is with purely commercial gain in mind. Where ethical businesses can gain a very real advantage is in widening their study and research programmes to include topics that are not directly related to their day-to-day activities. It is a long-term play, but one that adds value, brings competitive advantage and – most importantly – can help to instigate wider changes and improvements.

To offer a single instance of this, at Honey's we are developing a new set of nutritional guidelines for dogs. This will, we hope, replace the existing guidelines, which are published by various bodies such as the European Pet Food Industry Federation (FEDIAF) and the Association of American Feed Control Officials (AAFCO) and lack scientific validity. Our new guidelines will be of immense value to dog-lovers and also to all our competitors. Our main purpose is to disseminate our knowledge and we have little expectation of a sudden rush in custom. However, we do know that by sharing our expertise we will add to our credibility and this must, in turn, add value to our business.

PUBLISH A BOOK

THERE is no better way for an ethical business to establish its credentials and effect change than for one or more of its founders (ahem!) to publish a book.

Books (printed and digital) are an ideal way of reaching and influencing any target audience. Unlike, say, marketing material, books are viewed as being authoritative, independent and trustworthy. They are respected and they have – if you will excuse the pun – long shelf lives. Books are effective in two ways. Directly, when purchased by a reader and indirectly when:

- reported about as a news story
- written about – reviews, feature articles, references, blogs etc.

- talked about
- seen in shops and online.

Books serve another function. They can be used as the catalyst for other activities such as:

- social and media events – for instance, a launch party
- seminars
- television and radio programmes
- videos, podcasts and other online activity.

In short, there are substantial benefits to be obtained from publishing a book. In addition, the author of a book gains huge credibility.

A quick look online and you will see just how many ethical entrepreneurs have written books both about their businesses and about subjects that are important to them. This is the third book related to Honey's. The first was *Honey's Natural Feeding Handbook for Dogs* (by me) and the second was *The Lucky Dog Weight Loss Plan* (by Vicky). Neither makes much mention of our dog food company but focuses on providing readers with straightforward, accurate, hard-to-obtain nutritional advice for dogs and – to a lesser extent – cats. They can be purchased through any good bookshop and also online. We also offer a free download from our website and we donate copies for sale to any good canine cause that asks us. Our books have produced the following tangible benefits:

- We have helped tens of thousands (possibly more, it is hard to say) of people to switch their dog to a better diet.
- We have helped to promote better farm animal welfare.
- The books have been reviewed extensively in print and online.
- My book was used as the basis of a Channel 5 documentary about dog food.
- Vicky and I have both made countless appearances on radio talking about canine nutrition and other important subjects.
- We have been invited to write feature articles in lots of magazines and national newspapers.
- The books have been the basis of lectures given at universities, veterinary seminars and elsewhere.
- The books have provided content for our websites and other websites.

More than anything else, the work we put into

writing the books has helped to promote our beliefs and build our reputations. Not a day passes without someone mentioning to one or other of us that our books have altered their thought process or behaviour.

So much for the reasons why you should publish a book. How, if you are not a natural writer, are you to achieve it? Nothing could be simpler: employ a ghostwriter. You'll discover that there is no shortage of experienced journalists and authors only too willing to write, or help you write, your book. Whom you should approach will depend on your subject matter and budget. It could be that a local newspaper journalist will suit you perfectly, or an academic, or (if you can afford it) a better-known author.

What about the publication process? If you have a good story to tell you may be able to sell it to a publisher (with or without the help of a literary agent). Alternatively, you could publish it yourself. There are, happily, plenty of reference books and websites devoted to this very specialist topic. The most important point is that publishing a book will help your cause and your business.

SHOW YOUR CUSTOMERS YOU CARE

ONCE every week to ten days, I sit down and write to any Honey's customer who has lost a four-legged family member. Sometimes I handwrite a card, other times I type a letter and ask Charlotte or Oliver (my twelve-year-old twins) to decorate it and the envelope. Either way, I make reference to what we know about the dog or cat – its age, its health issues, how its death will affect other members of the family. If we have a photograph, I may write about that. I take the opportunity to thank the customer for his or her support and business. Each missive generally takes me between fifteen and thirty minutes. Often, I don't get to hear of a loss until months after it has happened, but I still try to write.

BY YOUR ACTIONS
SHALL YE BE
KNOWN...
**IF YOU
CARE**
ABOUT YOUR
CUSTOMERS,
YOU NEED TO
COME UP WITH
**TANGIBLE
WAYS** OF
SHOWING IT.

My condolence letters are important for two reasons. I know from first-hand experience that the loss of a dog or cat can be felt every bit as keenly as the loss of a human. I only have to think of some of the animals with whom I have been fortunate enough to share my life – even if they have been dead for decades – to tear up. However, those who grieve for animals often grieve alone as many of their friends and relatives may not understand the depth of their emotions. I am writing, then, as a fellow sufferer. I am also writing because I want to remind our own staff of the importance of thinking about our customers not as customers but as people.

When Vicky and I discuss any aspect of the way in which Honey's operates, we put ourselves in the position of a customer and try to imagine what would make us happy. The ways in which we demonstrate our commitment to our customers include:

• Making sure that all our customers have **my personal email address** in case they want to get directly in touch about anything.

• **Surprising** all our customers with little gifts. We've sent them everything from a little bottle of rescue remedy for animals to bars of hand-made soap, and from packets of dog treats to fridge magnets.

• If a customer does **something nice** for us (such as mention us on an online forum) and we happen to hear about it (and remember), we try to do something nice for them – such as giving them some free food or free delivery or some other perk.

• We keep a supply of **delicious, organic chocolate** in the office and we send a bar to customers we want to thank or apologize to.

• We ask our customers whether there is any **good cause** they support that they would like us to support.

• We ask for **photographs of the animals** we are feeding because we like to see what they look like – and because we are dogcentric, like many of our customers.

• We set aside **time to chat with customers** by phone and to correspond with them.

These are only a few examples, but I hope that they give a sense of our approach and philosophy. By your actions shall ye be known, and all that. Lots of big companies bang on about how they are customer-focused but it is rarely true. If you care about your customers, you need to come up with tangible ways of showing it. Incidentally, one of the great advantages of cultivating this sort of relationship with your customers is that they are more likely to be understanding when something goes wrong or you need a favour.

HOW TO TURN YOUR CUSTOMERS INTO FRIENDS

WHAT are the badges of true friendship? Mutual affection? Respect? Common interests? These and other factors can also be applied to an acquaintance. To my mind, a true friendship can only exist where confidences have been exchanged, sacrifices (or at least compromises) made and experiences shared. We know a great deal about our friends – even quite new friends – and it informs our relationship with them.

You might think that I am overstating it to propose that your customers also ought to be your friends, but I feel we manage it at Honey's. Taking the three criteria above, here are some examples of how we achieve it:

- **Exchange of confidences**. Our first telephone contact with a customer may last anything up to an hour during which time we will discuss their dog, its health, diet, likes and dislikes, exercise regime and personality. In the course of the conversation we often hear about our customer's life, work, family, home, health, financial circumstances and relationships. As it is a dialogue the customer, in turn, will find out a great deal about Honey's (our food, ethics, service, prices and so forth) as well as about whoever they are talking to, and about Vicky and me as founders of the business.

- **Sacrifices and compromises**. Honey's is not always an easy or convenient company to deal with. Our phone answering (if we are busy in the kitchens we may have to switch to the answering machine), lack of online ordering, environmentally friendly packaging etc., all mean a certain level of inconvenience for our customers. Even our staunchest allies could not describe us as a slick organization! But it is a two-way street, as we make compromises, too. For example, we sacrifice extra sales (through our policy of never bothering or pushing our customers) and profits (through our policy of slim margins).

• **Shared experiences**. These come in many forms. There are virtual shared experiences, for example, when we help a customer with a poorly dog – something that can involve dozens of telephone calls and emails. And there are face-to-face shared experiences, such as when we meet customers at events or when we run a tour of Honey's HQ and kitchens.

Large companies can make their customers their friends but for some reason – stupidity, perhaps, or laziness – few seem to bother.

YOU CAN'T BUY REFERRALS, YOU HAVE TO EARN THEM

I am not saying that Honey's *never* advertises, but we don't advertise much. Occasionally, we take space in one of the dog magazines just to remind people we exist. We have found that the majority of customers who come to us via these advertisements rarely place more than one or two orders. Since we need five or six orders to break even on a new customer, advertising is obviously not good value for money.

A quick analysis of our best customers shows that all but a tiny percentage have come to us because they met someone connected with the company, read one of our books or were introduced by a third party. The referrals are generally made by existing customers, although some vets, veterinary nurses, behaviourists and other canine professionals do also recommend us. Naturally, we say thank you. If the introducer is a canine professional, we try to support their practice with free food, free books, referrals of our own, or in some other way. If the introducer is one of our existing customers, we send them a gift. The gifts change from time to time but at the moment it is an invention of Vicky's called the Honey's Superdog Towel/Cape Thingy, which she promotes thus:

> The idea is simplicity itself. You take one wet dog, slip the Superdog Towel/Cape Thingy over their head, fasten it under the tum and then either rub them dry or leave them to run around until they dry themselves. No more chasing after your muddy four-legged angel with a towel and no more mud splatters all over your clothes/ newly painted walls etc...
>
> Cool, eh? But how can you get your paws on one? If you felt that it wouldn't be compromising your principles to recommend a new customer to Honey's, we'd include one of the exclusive Superdog Towel/Cape Thingies

WORD OF MOUTH

IS THE RESULT OF HOW YOUR COMPANY BEHAVES EACH AND EVERY SINGLE DAY TO ITS CUSTOMERS, STAFF AND SUPPLIERS. YOU CAN'T BUY IT;

YOU CAN ONLY EARN IT.

(in an appropriate size) with your next order as a thank-you present... free of charge.

Please ask whoever you introduce to let us know that it was you who put them up to it and we'll do the rest. If you are worried that in their excitement at becoming a new customer they may forget to mention you, then by all means call or email to make sure that we know. This probably contravenes some Data Protection law but, whatever, we'll risk it.

As you can see, the system is a tad informal but it seems to work. Incidentally, several customers suggested that we produce a business card for them to pass on to people interested in raw feeding. We created a set of cards with witty dog cartoons on one side and the following text on the other:

I'd like to recommend Honey's

Honey's is a small, artisan, raw dog food producer. Raw dog food? Yes, because dogs are healthier and happier if they eat the same sort of diet they would enjoy if they lived in the wild. Honey's make it easy to switch to a raw diet and they only use free-range, organic and/or wild meat suitable for human consumption. Honey's is happy to provide free diet and health advice

even if you never plan to become a customer.
Please do mention my name.

One of the wonderful things about so many of
our customers knowing other customers is that it
makes Honey's feel like a club. It also puts extra
pressure on Vicky, me and the rest of our team.
We fret dreadfully about ever letting any of our
customers down because they are so good to us.
As I mentioned earlier, running Honey's is a humbling experience and nowhere is this exemplified
better than in the matter of referrals.

Marketing gurus talk all the time about the
power of 'word of mouth' as if it is something
that can be achieved easily and quickly. Word of
mouth is actually the result of how your company
behaves each and every single day to its customers,
staff and suppliers. You can't buy it; you can only
earn it.

ETHICAL MARKETING'S GOLDEN RULES

I once asked the receptionist on the information desk at the Oxford Street branch of John Lewis where I would find moth balls and she answered, quick as a flash: 'Between his legs but if you want to commit murder moth foul I suggest the basement, laundry supplies, next to the kitchen department. Ask for David, he's our expert.' That the receptionist had a sense of humour and knew so much about the shop that she could direct me to the right department and name the person I should talk to without having to look it up, says everything about the John Lewis Group.

The John Lewis Group is run as a partnership and all the staff have a voice in its management and receive a share of its profits. No one earns sales commission. It is one of the largest private businesses in the UK with over 30 department stores, 350 Waitrose supermarkets and an enormous online presence. My family have been customers of John Lewis since the 1920s. I was taken there as a baby and I must have been in and out of its various shops several thousand times.

It is one of the few businesses remaining in the UK that offers employees a lifelong career. The staff are sometimes eccentric (once, when I was choosing a new double mattress, a member of the bedding department pretended to sleep on the other side of the bed so that I could get a better feel for the level of support), but they are always polite, well-informed, trustworthy and impartial. If you want to understand what you are buying and the various options open to you, there is no better place to go. For the last century or so the group's motto has been: 'Never Knowingly Undersold'. They take this promise seriously and will often telephone their competitors before you make a purchase in order to ensure that it isn't available elsewhere at a lower price. If it is, they drop their own price.

I have not signed up to the John Lewis loyalty scheme (which rewards its best customers with benefits such as free afternoon tea three times a year) because I don't need any other reason to shop there. I am on their mailing list but if they never contacted me with offers or news again, I would still spend the same amount of money with them. More than this, I am perfectly happy to tolerate John Lewis making the odd cock-up. If they keep me waiting (as they are slightly inclined to do) or get a delivery wrong, what of it? They are kind people and only human and – crucially – when they apologize, I feel they mean it.

There isn't a company in the world that doesn't want its customers to feel about it the way I feel about the John Lewis Group. Many, especially the bigger ones, look to their internal and external marketing experts to generate greater loyalty. Marketing, after all, has a well-deserved reputation for taking advantage of consumers. Its practitioners are experts at obfuscation and persuasion. They know how to play on our fears, insecurities and desires. They are skilled in what to hide and what to reveal. It is in part due to effective marketing that companies continue to sell us products and services that are poor value, poor quality, bad for our health (mental and physical), damaging to the environment and exploitative of workers. However, if you are one of those businesses that

customers tolerate rather than love, clever marketing may be able to boost your sales and profits,
but it isn't going to bring about lasting improvements. Only a different business philosophy can
achieve that.

Which brings us, in a somewhat roundabout
way, to the subject of marketing an ethical business, which is exactly like marketing any other
business, but with one crucial exception: you
can – in fact, you must – be 100 per cent honest.
There is no room – and no need – for exaggeration,
manipulation or deviation from the truth. You
can tell it like it is because that is exactly what
your customers and potential customers want to
hear. Moreover, because you are looking to recruit
fellow travellers – people who share your beliefs
– you will probably find that you need to spend
much, much less time or money on marketing.
Your customers will, as a matter of course, tell their
friends, relatives and colleagues about your work.

Since I helped to found Honey's, I have developed eleven golden rules by which we run our
marketing. Although, to be frank, we aren't really
marketing, we are simply communicating.

———

MARKETING AN
ETHICAL BUSINESS
IS EXACTLY LIKE
MARKETING
ANY OTHER BUSINESS,
WITH ONE CRUCIAL
EXCEPTION:
YOU CAN – IN
FACT, YOU MUST –
BE 100%
HONEST.

Rule one: Educate your consumers

The buying process for anything – even something inconsequential such as a newspaper or a loaf of bread – is remarkably complex and is influenced by an unimaginable number of factors from early childhood experiences to price, and from the purchaser's mood to the state of the economy. In theory, the decision will be a logical one, but as behavioural economists (or anyone standing outside a fast-food restaurant) know, people don't always do what is best for them or others. Nevertheless, whether someone is spending a relatively small or a really substantial sum of money they will, to a greater or lesser extent, put thought into the purchase. Consumers are thinkers. In particular, they think about their own wants and needs, which will include all sorts of beliefs. This is fantastic news for ethical businesses.

If you provide your potential customers with information about your company, the principles by which you operate it and exactly what you have to offer – and if you give them an opportunity to understand their own role in the equation – then you will receive a positive response. Many years ago, there was a chain of discounted designer-clothing stores in the USA called SYMS that had as its slogan: 'An educated consumer is our best customer.' An educated consumer is interested in the long term not the short term; in value not cost. The first golden rule of all ethical marketing is, therefore, to educate consumers. If you do nothing else your marketing plan will be a triumph.

Rule two: Set wider objectives

There is a predictability to most marketing plans. They open, almost without exception, with a statement of the marketing objectives. In plain English, these are invariably to:

- Generate sales inquiries – or in the case of retail, visits.
- Convert inquirers/visitors to customers or clients.
- Increase customer/client value by selling them more of the same or something new.
- Retain customers and stop them taking their business elsewhere.

Often the marketing objectives will be accompanied by precise targets. Take, as a random example, Bentley Motors. What good is a sales inquiry to them if it doesn't come from someone with the wherewithal to cough up at least £160,000 for a car? Their marketing plan probably looks something like this:

- Generate 200,000 sales inquiries from multi-millionaires and chauffeur service companies worldwide.
- Arrange 50,000 test drives from qualified prospects worldwide.
- Sell a car to one-in-five people who take a test drive – i.e. 10,000 cars a year.
- Optimize the number of Bentley owners who need their cars serviced – a very profitable line for car manufacturers and dealers.
- Ensure that existing owners choose Bentley for their next new car.

At Honey's we take a slightly different view. Our marketing objectives are identical to our business objectives, viz. to encourage dog-lovers to switch their four-legged charges to a raw diet and to campaign for better treatment of farm animals. We hope that a percentage of those we introduce to raw feeding and/or who share our anger over farm animal exploitation will either become customers or recommend us to someone else.

So far it is working and as a result we don't have to waste any time thinking about how many inquiries we receive or whether they become customers or persuading them to spend more with us. We don't have to take any special action to try to keep our customers locked in to us, either. We have found that if a Honey's customer stops buying from us it is, with a handful of exceptions, because they no longer have a dog, have decided to make their own dog food, or for some other reason that is unconnected to our service or food quality. Whatever their reason for leaving, we respect it. We generally telephone them just to make sure we haven't done something wrong, but we don't insult them by trying to lure them back with special offers or extra service.

In a nutshell: traditional marketing objectives are limiting and tantamount to an admission that a business has to talk its customers into buying from them.

Rule three: Don't waste time on identifying typical customers

Marketing manuals place great emphasis on understanding your target audience. Some will suggest you draw up little 'word pictures' to describe your customers and what motivates them. Others will urge you to focus on demographic information such as their gender, income, marital status and location.

Ethical business owners need not trouble themselves with any of this.

Take a typical Honey's customer. Those with just one Honey's-fed dog will spend an average of £80 a month with us. Many, of course, feed more than one dog and so spend more. You might assume, therefore, that the majority of our customers are worth a few bob and live in posh areas. You'd be wrong. A surprisingly high percentage of Honey's customers earn the average UK income or less, and more than a few of them reside in mobile homes. However, they do share certain characteristics. These are that they all:

- love dogs
- have inquiring, open minds
- are kind
- are concerned about social issues
- are animal-lovers.

Beyond that it would be dangerous to try to pigeonhole them. We feed the dogs of those who are young and old, city- and country-dwellers, believers and agnostics, left- and right-wing voters... In short, anything but a homogenous group. By and large, customers of ethical businesses tend to be non-conformist. There is little point in trying to categorize them.

Rule four: Ethical businesses have no competitors

It is widely believed to be good policy to research your competition – the technical term for this is gaining 'competitive intelligence'. If you are setting up a genuinely ethical business this may be easier said than done. Purely profit-driven companies can hardly be counted as competitors, since their core philosophy will be so completely and utterly different from your own. Any socially responsible enterprise in the same sector ought to be your friends, not your rivals. Obviously, it makes sense to study and learn from companies engaged in providing similar products or services and you may want to investigate their prices or some other aspect of their operation. Arrogant as it will sound, however, I wouldn't waste too much time looking at what other businesses are doing. Better to focus on what you believe to be important.

Rule five: Pricing can always be changed

Pricing a new product or service is complicated. You need to consider not just the amount of money that is required to cover your production and distribution costs, but also what you need to pay for all your other expenses – many of which may be related to your wider, not-for-profit objectives. Honey's food, for example, would cost less if we didn't choose to fund charity work, research, campaigning, a free advisory service, free or discounted sample food and so forth. On the other hand, we would have to charge more if we wanted to invest in 'conventional' practices such as advertising or distribute our food through retailers. The price of our ethical liver treats – Beautiful Joe's – has to cover not just our manufacturing, packaging and distribution costs (we are obliged to give a 50 per cent wholesale discount to get into shops), but also our one-for-one donations, whereby we give away half of what we sell to rescue charities.

DON'T WASTE TOO MUCH **TIME** LOOKING AT WHAT OTHER BUSINESSES ARE DOING – **FOCUS ON WHAT *YOU* BELIEVE** TO BE IMPORTANT.

Given the above, you may not get it right from day one. Which is why it's worth remembering that whether you are selling direct to your customers or through a third party, it is always possible to change your prices later.

Rule six: Prioritize your messages

What do you want to tell your customers and prospective customers about your business? If you visit the Newman's Own website you'll see that the main headline is a quote from the late Paul Newman: 'Let's give it all away to those who need it.' Underneath this message you have a choice. You can learn about the Newman's Own products – pasta sauces, salad dressings, salsa and other foodstuffs – or its charitable foundation. Interestingly, if you opt to learn about the products, you will still encounter lots of messages making it clear that all the profits from the business – which was established by Paul Newman and an author called A. E. Hotchner – go to charity.

With an ethical business, there is generally a great deal to say. At Honey's, for example, we want to tell people about raw feeding (which is still relatively unknown), our food, our policy regarding sourcing, our free advisory service, our certified organic status, our special offers and a host of other important subjects. The result is that our communications tend to contain a great number of words and look quite busy. Generally speaking, companies try and make all their marketing material conform to certain copy and design guidelines, so that it is instantly recognizable. Honey's doesn't bother with all that guff. Our attitude is that we are a small, artisan dog food producer and if we look a little amateur – well, we are a little amateur, what of it?

One of the most fruitful marketing activities you can undertake is to write down, in plain English, a summary of all the information you want to give your customers and prospective customers. When I am carrying out this sort of exercise I tend to draw up two columns – one with features and the other with benefits. Features are, basically, descriptive (for example, organic surface cleaner), while benefits are emotional (cleans better and harmless to the environment). Then I rank the list in terms of importance. Next, I consider any offer I want to make – such as 'buy one get one free' – any time restrictions – 'buy now before the VAT increase' – and any other factors worthy of mention.

Having such a list will make all your communication efforts easier and more effective.

Rule seven: Choose your media with care

Having established to whom you want to talk and what you want to tell them, you need to decide the best way to reach them. Your options can be divided into:

Advertising

You will be paying someone else – such as a newspaper, television or radio station – to communicate your message for you.

Direct response

Whatever communication you devise will be designed to achieve a measurable response – such as someone placing an order or telephoning for more information.

Public relations (PR)

You'll be hoping to get someone else – invariably a journalist – to communicate your message for you. It can also include other activities – such as events and books.

Sales promotion
Whereby you encourage your audience to make a purchase by offering them an incentive.

Packaging, print and design
Whereby you use your product packaging, printed material and design to communicate your message.

In terms of actual media, you have the choice of:

Broadcast media
Television and radio commercials.

Print media
Newspapers, magazines, books, direct mailings, newsletters and so forth.

Outdoor media
Billboards, posters, signage etc.

Digital media
Websites, social media – such as Facebook, Twitter and blogs – email, SMS and so forth.

Experiential media

Events, trade shows, exhibitions and other one-to-one encounters that are related to an actual experience.

Alternative media

Everything from display stands in supermarkets to the back of car park tickets.

John Wanamaker, an American businessman, once complained: 'Half the money I spend on advertising is wasted. The trouble is, I don't know which half.' If anything, he was understating the size of the problem. I would guess that as much as 90 per cent of all advertising – or to be more accurate, marketing – is wasted. For this reason, I recommend starting with the bare minimum and gradually testing new media over time.

At Honey's we began with a website (built by my twenty-one-year-old son) and a small brochure, which we handed out at dog shows and country fairs. This got us started. I wrote my book about canine nutrition and the publicity from that was a great help. Much, much later on we tried a couple of advertisements, created a leaflet for vets and also started a Facebook page. After that Vicky's book about weight loss for dogs was published. Most recently of all we have made a number of videos. Over the years, there have been plenty of fact sheets and fliers, but when I look through our archives it has to be said that we have created very few pure marketing items.

I suspect that an ethical business's media requirements are less than those of a purely profit-driven business. Why? Because its customers are spreading the word on their behalf.

Rule eight: Never think of your business as a 'brand'

Our brand this, our brand that, our brand message, building our brand, our brand values, creating our brand... Marketing people have become obsessed with the whole concept of 'brand'. No one can agree, however, what they mean by it. The American Marketing Association, for example, defines it as:

> A **name, term, design, symbol, or any other feature** that identifies one seller's good or service as distinct from those of other sellers.

> The legal term for brand is **trademark**. A brand
> may identify one item, a family of items, or all
> items of that seller. If used for the firm as a
> whole, the preferred term is trade name.

Whereas Seth Godin, a journalist, feels that a brand: '... Is the set of expectations, memories, stories and relationships that, taken together, account for a consumer's decision to choose one product or service over another.'

Paul Biedermann, a marketing consultant, describes a brand as: '... The essence of one's own unique story. This is as true for personal branding as it is for business branding. The key, though, is reaching down and pulling out the authentic, unique "you".'

For my own part, I feel that the advertising expert David Meerman Scott comes closer to it, when he says: 'Branding is what lazy and ineffective marketing people do to occupy their time and look busy.'

Instinctively, I am against the idea of thinking of a business as a brand, partly because I hate unnecessary jargon and partly because it depersonalizes what you are doing.

———

Rule nine: Your best customer may or may not be your existing customer

There is an old marketing adage that your best customer is your existing customer. It is not without some validity. If someone knows and loves your business and is buying from you regularly then, of course, you want to put them first and keep them happy. It is why, for example, so many businesses invest in expensive loyalty programmes and bombard their customers with information and special offers.

However, there is a downside to focusing too much on your existing customers.

Customers are people. They lead complicated lives. Whatever you are providing them with – even if it is something vital such as, ahem, organic raw dog food – could temporarily or permanently become less important to them. For example, they could experience a change in their personal circumstances, including a reduced income. Putting all your marketing eggs into one basket – existing customers – is all well and good, but it may leave your business vulnerable.

Moreover, really good customers rarely materialize from nowhere. They have to be found and

REALLY GOOD CUSTOMERS RARELY MATERIALIZE FROM NOWHERE. THEY HAVE TO BE FOUND AND NURTURED.

nurtured. One of the benefits of the Honey's policy of providing free expert canine nutrition advice and information to anyone who approaches us is that it ensures that we are always in contact with plenty of new people. It is also a benefit of the books we publish, and the heavily discounted sample food we provide to people who want to try raw feeding their dogs.

There is no such thing as a 'best customer'. Customers and prospective customers are of equal value and deserve to be treated as such.

Rule ten: Don't make it too easy for your customers

We give away a great deal for free at Honey's, including all the information you need to make your own raw dog food. If you want to sample our food, however, you must pay us. We say – and it is true – that this is because our ingredient and delivery costs are so high. But there is another reason. By charging our prospective customers for sample food we ensure that they are serious about raw feeding. It gives our food (and service) more value.

Rule eleven: Go for the low-hanging fruit

It is tempting, when weighing up different marketing and communication options, to be lured into activities that are time-consuming and/or expensive and/or not that effective.

To offer one example, we'd like to see more vets understanding raw feeding and – hopefully – referring patients to our highly qualified Health Team, but we have discovered that trying to reach vets, get their attention, persuade them to open their minds to species-appropriate diets and remind them we offer free support to anyone who wants to contact us is an almost pointless task. On the other hand, we get on very well with homoeopathic vets who are, by and large, open-minded and much more in tune with our own beliefs and philosophies. So, we focus our efforts not on vets as a whole, but on homoeopathic vets. There are fewer than one hundred of them but some may send as many as fifty or sixty dog-lovers a year to us.

To offer another example, we know that when we create a video about raw feeding and post it on Facebook, it may receive up to 10,000 or more views in a matter of days. We know, too, that such videos help to widen the public's understanding of raw feeding, farm animal welfare and other subjects close to our hearts. Also, we are the only ethical dog food producer in the world creating well-researched, impartial videos. Worth doing, then. To make even a short video costs over £1,000 and takes up to three or four days. For this reason, we postponed making videos until we had reached a certain size and could afford the time and expense.

In general, for any business – ethical or otherwise – it is more efficient to go for quicker, less costly, more responsive marketing activities.

PLAN FOR LONGEVITY

HOW long do you expect your business to survive? During the 1950s, the average age of a US public company was sixty-one years. Currently, it is around eighteen years and falling. One in three public companies will have failed or merged with another company within the next five years. Start-ups fail at a considerably faster rate – in the UK barely half ever celebrate their fifth birthdays. Whilst human life expectancy has been growing, business life expectancy has been declining.

It doesn't have to be like this. There are plenty of companies that survive and prosper for hundreds of years. The Japanese have a surprising number of businesses over 1,000 years old, including a hotel that opened its doors in 705. Indeed, there are so many long-established businesses in Japan that they have a special word to describe them: *shinise*. The Swedish word for business, incidentally, is *näringslivet*, which translates as 'nourishment for life', while the ancient Chinese character for commerce can be translated as 'survive' and 'birth'.

If you take a strictly utilitarian, market-driven approach to business, then, of course, short life expectancy is perfectly acceptable. An opportunity exists or is created, a business seizes it, the opportunity ends, the business closes or is merged with another business. Leaving aside enterprises that fail through poor management or circumstances beyond their control, short-lived businesses that rise and then crash are unlikely to be engaged in activities of real value to the world. Rather, they are machines to make money.

What can you do to ensure the longevity of your own business? Arie de Geus, the former head of strategic planning at Royal Dutch Shell and author of an excellent book called *The Living Company*, believes that businesses are living things and that they die because they place too little emphasis on learning. According to him, companies must invest in research, education and training if they want to survive. De Geus also points out that one of the features of successful companies is that they are not afraid to change their main line of business when required. Nokia, now known as a technology company, started out life as a pulp mill and has been involved in a wide variety of other activities from lavatory paper to gas masks since it was founded in 1865. De Geus says: 'The ability to learn faster than your competitors may be the only sustainable competitive advantage.'

Martin Reeves, a biologist turned business strategist, has a different perspective. He has proposed that businesses that want to survive indefinitely should turn to nature and model themselves along the lines of the human immune system. He identifies various features of the immune system that businesses would do well to replicate, including diversity, a modular structure (if one thing fails, another takes over), adaptivity, prudence and embeddedness (being part of something larger). To his mind almost all businesses make the mistake of being mechanical in their approach. They set goals, analyse problems, construct and adhere to plans, and concentrate on being effective, all in a relatively short time frame. He says that this is a good strategy in a stable, unchanging environment but that the moment such a business is challenged it is lost. He uses lots of examples to illustrate his theories, including the failure of

Kodak at a time when its closest competitor, Fuji, was thriving.

Entrepreneurs tend to divide into two groups. There are those who are less committed to what they are doing and have one eye on an exit strategy from the beginning. And then there are those who are completely and utterly in love with their creations and can't bear the idea of being parted from them. Vicky and I fall into the latter category. We are on a mission. I would like to leave the meat business eventually, as I have already explained. Vicky may also decide, one day, that she wants to put her energy into something else. But the business is run on the basis that we will be its shareholders for ever. Decisions are made for the long term – the very long term. As a result, we believe we are building a much, much stronger business.

GROWTH IS NOT EVERYTHING

THE world has become obsessed with growth. Countries, regions, cities and, of course, businesses are judged to a great extent on whether or not they are expanding and – if they are – at what rate. The irony of this is that growth depends on the exploitation of resources – both human and natural. So, as we expand, we destroy.

It is difficult not to think of large businesses – especially multinationals – in a negative way. They are difficult to manage, wasteful, out of touch with their stakeholders and often morally suspect. Few have much of a personality. None is humble. They lack humanity. To my mind, society would be better served if all businesses were small- to medium-sized.

Obviously, if a business doesn't grow during its early stages it won't ever become economically viable. Once a business reaches profitability and is showing a consistent and reasonable return on investment, I suspect many shareholders would be perfectly happy if it neither grew nor shrank. Unfortunately, and I speak here from personal experience, such a delicate balance is almost impossible to achieve. Businesses that aren't getting larger are vulnerable to becoming smaller. So, in a way, business sustainability is inevitably linked to continued growth.

For most businesses, growth ought to represent extra profits, all things being equal, but for an ethical business, growth offers opportunities to achieve its other aims.

For example, PatientsLikeMe is a patient network and real-time research platform. In plain English, it is a free-to-use website where patients connect with others who have the same disease or condition and track and share their own experiences. In the process, they generate data about the real-world nature of disease. With nearly 500,000 members, PatientsLikeMe has become a huge information resource and has published more than eighty research studies. It was started by James and Ben Heywood, who lost their brother to amyotrophic lateral sclerosis – a form of motor neurone disease – and it describes itself as a 'for-profit company with a not-just-for-profit attitude'. It makes its money from research partnerships, grants and selling anonymous data. The more profit it can make, the more patients it can connect and the more medical solutions it can help develop.

We have never tracked Honey's growth in percentage terms. Initially, it must have been massive because we went from nothing to a £1 million turnover relatively quickly. There was then something of a hiatus, before an extremely dramatic growth spurt. The latter was brought about by a television documentary on dog food in which we featured strongly.

Actually, to say we featured strongly is a bit of an understatement. The head of the production company that made the programme was a customer of ours. When he asked me to help him plan a documentary about dog food, I pointed out that no commercial television station would commission what he intended because they depended on dog food manufacturers for a big slug of their advertising revenue (the BBC, for reasons I have never been able to ascertain, just isn't that interested in dog food). I was right and wrong.

He made his pitch to several channels and was turned down by all of them. Then, unexpectedly, a new controller was appointed to Channel 5 who happened to have met me at a party and had read my canine nutrition book. He said that, against his better instincts, he would fund the programme.

Ultimately, the programme was heavily edited so as not to offend any advertisers. Nevertheless, it was still highly critical of processed dog food manufacturers and positive about raw feeding. Vicky and I were in it, but our company name was barely mentioned. This suited the makers (who were, after all, customers and didn't want to appear biased) and us (who were more interested in winning hearts than wallets). Four days before the programme aired, the *Daily Mail* published a feature article by me about species-appropriate diets for dogs, and from seven o'clock that morning we were inundated with inquirers.

Honey's would normally expect to receive a handful of inquiries every day from dog-lovers interested in learning more about raw feeding. The morning the *Daily Mail* article ran, we received over 500 emails and phone calls. We are not sure how many inquiries we received over the next fortnight – it was impossible to keep count – but it ran to thousands.

As you can imagine we were both thrilled and appalled. On the one hand, we had helped to make raw feeding topical and, despite doing nothing to promote ourselves, a huge number of dog-lovers had managed to track us down. On the other hand, if everyone who worked for Honey's did nothing else for eight hours a day, six days a week (i.e. if we stopped making the food, looking after existing customers etc.), we estimated it would take a year to speak to everyone who had contacted us.

We considered various strategies, such as employing an external sales team and introducing online ordering, but decided against them. Our predominant goal was to promote raw feeding, not to optimize our own sales. Instead, we apologized to everyone who had contacted us for not being able to respond immediately, sent them free information and promised to provide a quotation as soon as possible as long as they let us have the necessary details about their dog(s). Those who were serious were happy to wait. We probably grew by about 20 per cent as a result of the publicity, which was a fraction of what we could have achieved if we had adopted a more commercial approach. We didn't care because we believe that growth is not everything.

YOU CAN'T PLEASE EVERYONE

THERE are lots of people Honey's has annoyed. Anyone who thinks that processed dog food is healthier for dogs than raw dog food. Anyone who doesn't believe it is possible to communicate with animals. Anyone who doesn't believe in homoeopathy. Anyone who insists we owe them commission for recommending our food. Anyone who doesn't agree that dogs are over-vaccinated. The list is long and varied. One would think that being an ethical business we would be beloved by one and all, but that hasn't entirely been our experience. In fact, we often seem to polarize opinion. Holding strong beliefs is not universally good for business. However, it just isn't possible to please everyone and we aren't interested in trying.

CUSTOMER DATABASES ARE NOT THE WORK OF THE DEVIL

MY family and I love to shop in Fuller's, Union Hall, which is close to where we live in West Cork, Ireland. When I was first taken there in the 1960s, Fuller's was a grocer, general store and builders' merchant. A neighbour says that back then she overheard a customer ask for: 'Half a pound of butter, eight rashers of bacon, a dozen six-inch nails, a mousetrap and a shroud.'

The shop is no longer quite the Aladdin's cave it once was, but the Fullers (it has been in the same family since 1828) still blend their own tea, offer a quirky selection of books and maintain a hardware section. It is perfectly possible to nip in and out of the shop without saying a word to anyone, but we generally stop to chat. We know everyone who works there (they are our neighbours, after all) and they know us. You can serve yourself or one of the staff will fetch what you want. Either way, your shopping will be packed and carried out to your car or, if you live in the village, dropped at your door. You will, as a matter of course, always be earnestly thanked for your custom.

Noel and Ingrid Fuller, the current proprietors, are particularly good at anticipating their regulars' needs. For example, one October I mentioned that our oldest son would be coming home for Christmas. Without having to be asked, Noel went out of his way to find and stock a particular brand of biscuits that he knew Nat liked and he also remembered to keep a copy of Nat's favourite newspaper for him every day over the holidays.

Most of us yearn to be recognized by the businesses we give our custom to. Even minor acknowledgements can be gratifying. I am always pleased when anyone serving me – a cashier, for example, or a waiter – refers to me by name, especially when it is unprompted. I am most loyal to enterprises that make me feel I am remembered and appreciated. For a business with a relatively small clientele such as Fuller's, it is relatively easy

JUST BECAUSE **BIG, GREEDY, PROFIT-DRIVEN, EXPLOITATIVE** BUSINESSES USE TECHNOLOGY TO MANAGE THEIR CUSTOMER RELATIONSHIPS DOESN'T MEAN **SMALLER, GENEROUS, PRINCIPLE-DRIVEN, ETHICAL** BUSINESSES SHOULDN'T AS WELL.

to create lasting, meaningful customer relationships. For a larger business, however, the task
is considerably harder, which is why, without
exception, they all employ customer relationship
management (CRM) systems.

A CRM is a computer database containing each
customer's details plus contact and sales history.
Most CRMs include scripts and prompts so that
the employees know exactly what to say or write to
the customer in any given situation. To check that
employees are following instructions when they
talk to customers, their supervisors are able to listen
in and almost without exception calls are recorded.
It is difficult to imagine an approach more likely to
demotivate employees and annoy customers. How
can two people build a relationship, after all, if one
person is reciting someone else's words and both
parties are conscious that everything they say may
be listened to at a later date?

Anyway, just because big, greedy, profit-driven,
exploitative businesses use technology to manage
their customer relationships doesn't mean smaller,
generous, principle-driven, ethical businesses
shouldn't. When Vicky and I found that we could
no longer sustain daily contact with all of our
customers we invested in a highly sophisticated
database that we call WOOF. It was built to our

own specification and it holds not only the usual contact, order and payment information, but also a wealth of detail about the dogs we are feeding – everything from their date of birth to the name of their vet – as well as photographs where we have them. It is what allows us to offer our customers the same sort of high-quality service provided by Fuller's in Union Hall, which should be the golden standard by which all customer service is judged.

DON'T LET OTHER PEOPLE FREAK YOU OUT

WE don't own the platform on which our customer database is held. It is the property of a local IT developer called Matt who works on his own and from home.

At one point, we were persuaded by a colleague – acting from the best of motives – that being dependent on one person and not owning the database made Honey's vulnerable. They painted a terrifically convincing picture to Vicky and me of the whole company folding as a result of some disaster (mental or physical) befalling Matt. We were doubtful, so we asked someone else with more experience for advice. They concurred. We became so rattled that we pretty much dropped everything else we were doing to try to find a solution.

After a certain amount of external consultation we decided the best plan would be to commission our own platform that would replicate and improve upon Matt's work. We obtained a quotation of £3,000 and were given a time frame of twelve weeks.

Unfortunately, both the budget and the time frame proved unrealistic. As three months became six months and six months a year – and as the cost mounted – we kept reminding ourselves how vital the project was.

It was only after we had spent over thirty times the original budget and marked the project's second anniversary that we pulled the plug.

Yes, our customer database could be quicker and more powerful. Yes, there is a risk associated with being dependent on a small, external supplier.

However, the reality is that the existing database works perfectly well and even if the worst happened and we lost all access to our platform Honey's would survive. Or not.

We learnt our lesson: don't let other people's insecurities freak you out.

THE BIGGEST RISK YOU FACE IS REGRET

THERE is another subject, not unconnected with insecurity and fear, that I want to raise. My father, an academic, was horrified when I went into trade. 'For heaven's sake be careful,' he warned me. 'There are an awful lot of sharks in business and you could well lose all your money.' He assumed, which I suppose was a sort of compliment, that I would never be the cause of my own business downfall, but that it would be unscrupulous competitors who would do for me. At any rate, his first thought when I told him I was starting up on my own was to imagine defeat and failure. In fact, up until the day he died, his oft repeated mantra (after 'I do wish you had gone to Oxford

YOU CAN EARN
AN INFINITE
AMOUNT OF
MONEY DURING
YOUR LIFE,

BUT NOTHING
WILL ALTER THE
FACT THAT YOU
ONLY HAVE
**A FINITE
AMOUNT**
OF TIME.

or even, at a pinch, Cambridge') was: 'Business is terribly risky.'

If you start a business and things go horribly wrong, you will be amazed at how quickly you recover from your financial and emotional losses. I speak, let me assure you, with the voice of experience. The first time is the worst. There is a tendency to dwell on what might have been, the missing cash and one's bruised ego. However, there is also an extraordinary sense of relief and a sense that one is now free to try something else – something better. Anyway, you can earn an infinite amount of money during your life, but nothing will alter the fact that you only have a finite amount of time. Procrastinate about something you want to do – especially if it is something you really believe in – and you face the biggest risk of all: regret.

THE GREAT HONEY'S SURVEY

WE have only ever sent out one survey to our customers. It ran to eight full pages and required anything from fifteen minutes to well over an hour to complete, depending on the sort of detail the recipient wanted to go into – there were lots of open-ended questions.

When I created it, I hoped that one in twenty of our customers would answer it. In my wildest dreams, I imagined one in ten customers responding. What actually happened was that over half (52 per cent to be precise) of Honey's customers took the time to fill it in and return it.

There are, with the benefit of hindsight, a number of reasons why I think it was so successful:

Although we had never bothered our customers with a survey before, they were used to us asking them questions and knew we would act on their responses. For example, as I mentioned earlier, before we send even sample food to a new potential customer we ask all about the dog (or cat) we hope to be feeding including his or her name, age, gender, breed (if relevant), weight, health issues (if any), allergies, level of exercise, likes and dislikes and personality. The Honey's ethos is to ask questions and engage in a dialogue. The survey was an extension of this philosophy.

There was a clear reason for every single question and where necessary we explained why we were asking it. For example, we requested information about the customer's vet or vets so that (with permission) we could contact them if their dog ever had a health issue. We also asked if the vet (or vets) supported species-appropriate diets for dogs, as we are always being approached for referrals.

We guided customers through the survey with useful little notes.

It was a paper survey. Digital surveys are not Honey's style! We included a pen and reply-paid envelope so as to minimize the effort required.

We tried to make the survey entertaining. We called it 'The Great Honey's Survey' and included cartoons, illustrations and what I hope were witty little comments on every page. It came in a large envelope covered in cartoons and included a begging letter (there were pictures of dogs begging) 'from the basket of our pack leader: Vicky'.

We offered a thank-you present. In with each survey was a miniature box of chocolates to enjoy while answering the questions. Every completed survey was put into a draw for a whole year of free dog food – something worth winning.

It wasn't self-serving. That is to say, we asked for opinions, criticisms and ideas. We weren't trying to benchmark our performance. Our objective was purely and simply to deliver a better, more personal service to each and every customer.

When the responses began to flood in, we realized that we wouldn't be able to action all the different points immediately. Vicky decided that she would write a personal note to every respondent thanking them and explaining that due to the volume of completed surveys it could take a week or two to act on any requests they had made and/or to give them proper feedback.

With only a handful of exceptions our customers told us they were more than happy with
the products and service we were supplying. This
pleased us, of course. But it also had the effect of
making us even more determined never to let a
single customer down.

HOPE FOR THE BEST, PLAN FOR THE WORST

'THE pessimist complains about the wind; the optimist expects it to change; the realist adjusts the sails.' Not my own words, but William Arthur Ward's, and he makes a good point. Sooner or later your business, no matter how successful, no matter how worthy, will be confronted with unavoidable change. Some businesses – Xerox, BlackBerry, Blockbuster Video, Yahoo, Polaroid and pretty much every newspaper publisher in the world, to offer just a handful of examples – are so poorly prepared for change that they fail or as good as fail.

It would be nice to think that an ethical business – a business that is mindful of its stakeholders and the environment and which behaves in a decent, transparent manner – would be less vulnerable. If only it were true. At Honey's we spend a lot of time worrying about external factors that could bring about our demise and we have identified a variety of risks, including:

- **New regulations hampering the sale of raw dog food**. There are rumours that vested interests have been pressuring Defra and other regulatory bodies to ban or restrict the sale of raw dog food on the basis of questionable claims regarding food safety.

- **A major recession**. Because we use British free-range, wild and certified organic meat and organic vegetables suitable for human consumption, despite working on a slim margin, our food costs considerably more than the own-brand dried and canned food sold in supermarkets. Serious economic downturn could result in a serious loss of business.

- **Inability to source ingredients**. Only a small percentage of UK farms are free-range and an even smaller percentage are organic. As a result, we often find it tricky to source the ingredients we want. We also worry that an outbreak of disease, such as avian flu or foot and mouth, would make sourcing of certain ingredients impossible.

What about the risks we can't identify? Our solution is diversification. We have started four separate businesses since we founded Honey's. At the time of writing, one is in abeyance, one is modestly successful and two are still in development. All the businesses reflect our not-only-for-profit objectives:

- **Inventor's Notebook** is a one-for-one station-ery company. When you buy a notebook, we give a notebook to a child learning to read via the charity Room to Read. We attempted to launch this as a business-to-business enterprise, but although senior decision-makers in large public companies loved the idea, their stationery-buyers didn't. We have a warehouse full of rather beautiful handmade notebooks and when we get around to it, we plan to try selling them direct to consumers.

• **Beautiful Joe's is an ethical dog treat producer**. Every time we sell a packet of treats we give the same volume of treats to a rescue centre. This one-for-one model has been successful and the business would be profitable, only we keep giving away extra treats. We have plans to turn this into a much bigger one-for-one canine accessories business.

• **Vegetarian – maybe even vegan – raw dog food**. Although dogs are much healthier on a predominantly raw meat diet, they are well able to lead normal, healthy lives on a non-meat diet. Many vegetarians and vegans want nothing to do with meat even if they know it is ethically sourced and beneficial for their dogs. We have been experimenting with creating a range of nutritiously adequate vegetarian and vegan raw dog food recipes.

• **Wild and Precious**. New babies born in the USA or Europe have over 220 man-made chemicals in their bloodstreams – a large per-centage of which come from skincare products, toiletries, make-up and household cleaning agents. A growing number of doctors believe that these products are one of the causes for the increased cancer rate. A number of years ago, we set out to create a range of products that didn't use a single man-made chemical but only natural, organic ingredients. Lots of producers make this claim but their lists of ingredients tell another story.

We have invested a considerable amount of time and effort into these businesses but we haven't allowed them to distract us too much from our main objective, which is to spread the word about raw feeding and promote better farm animal welfare. Although we hope that in the fullness of time each will turn out to be successful, their purpose is to ensure that we don't get caught out if Honey's encounters some unforeseen disaster.

Some businesses, like some people, stick to one thing, never face a serious external challenge and prosper. Because they focus all their efforts on one area and don't allow themselves to be distracted they are able to grow much faster. It may appear that they are cleverer than those of us who find our businesses or careers overtaken by events, new technology or some other factor such as changing consumer opinion. It is more likely that they are simply luckier. It is not the strongest of the species that survives, nor the most intelligent, but the one most responsive to change. Not my own, but Charles Darwin's, and he makes a good point.

PERSISTENCE IS A MISUNDERSTOOD VIRTUE

MY late uncle Robert – a self-made American advertising millionaire – believed that persistence was the most important attribute to possess if one wanted to succeed. All of his stories, whether they related to winning a client or winning a game of golf, were based on the premise that all one had to do to achieve one's goals was to keep on trying. I believed him and for much of my life prided myself on my tenacity. In business, this often meant that I persisted with an idea long after someone not imbued with the same sense of determination would have chucked it in. How much better off I would have been if I had followed W. C. Fields's advice: 'If at first you don't succeed, try, try again. Then give up. There's no use in being a damn fool about it.'

When I consider the few really successful business projects I have been involved with, once I started telling prospective customers about them, they took off really quickly. But every lemon I came up with was a hard sell from day one, and if I had been more astute, I would have seen this at the time. Persistence is an invaluable but misunderstood virtue: it needs to be applied to innovation and improvement, not to something that isn't working and won't ever work.

A BIT OF FLAUNTING
NEVER GOES AMISS

DURING my wilderness years – I refer to the time I spent in advertising – I talked up the size of my business. I pretended we had more clients, more staff, more offices and higher sales than we did. Even when we reached quite a decent size, employing around a hundred staff across four locations, I was inclined to exaggerate. At that time, in that industry, size really mattered.

I have changed and so has the world. Big businesses – especially multinationals – are now viewed with deep (and generally justified) suspicion. Every year Edelman, a PR company, publishes a 'Trust Barometer' and one of its consistent findings (also reflected by other surveys) is that consumers trust big corporations less and less. In fact, barely at all.

IF YOU
ARE RUNNING A
SMALL,
LOCAL,
ARTISANAL AND
ETHICAL BUSINESS
YOUR
TIME HAS
COME.

This probably accounts for why so many big companies are trying to appear other than they are. A good example is Dorset Cereals. Read their packaging or look at their website and you could be forgiven for thinking that here is a tiny, British, artisan producer run by one man with a passion for organic muesli. Dig very slightly deeper (for example, by looking at the company's Wikipedia page) and you will see that while this may have been the case in 1989 when Dorset Cereals was founded, today it is owned by Associated British Foods, which has a turnover of £12,800 million a year.

If you are running a small, local, artisanal and ethical business your time has come. My advice is to flaunt it.

KNOW WHEN YOU HAVE HAD ENOUGH

IT is exciting to start and run any business, but especially an ethical business where success also means achieving some higher purpose.

However, there is a downside.

It is only too easy, and I speak here from experience, to become obsessed with the idea of more. I have a feeling that this is what inspired Thomas Traherne, the seventeenth-century poet, to write:

> When I came into the country and being seated among silent trees, had all my Time in my own hands, I resolved to spend it all, whatever it cost me, in the search for happiness and to satiate

that burning thirst which Nature had enkindled
in me from my youth.

Kurt Vonnegut summed it up well, too, in this
poem (published in the *New Yorker* in 2005) about
his late friend, Joseph Heller:

Joe Heller
True story, Word of Honor:
Joseph Heller, an important and funny writer
now dead,
and I were at a party given by a billionaire
on Shelter Island.

I said, 'Joe, how does it make you feel
to know that our host only yesterday
may have made more money
than your novel *Catch-22*
has earned in its entire history?'
And Joe said, 'I've got something he can never have.'
And I said, 'What on earth could that be, Joe?'
And Joe said, 'The knowledge that I've got enough.'
Not bad! Rest in peace!

No one else is ever likely to tell you that you have enough – enough money, enough material objects, enough work – so, you will need to watch for the moment yourself.

IT IS GOOD TO BE EMOTIONAL

I admire and respect everyone who works for Honey's and I love (although I would never say anything to them) several of the team. I love all our customers and I especially love all their dogs. I love all the many different people from vets to journalists who so generously support us. I love the charities we support and the fact that we can support them. I love my work. I love the modest difference that we are, hopefully, managing to make.

Before you find yourself retching, I should also add that I love annoying the greedy, hypocritical, self-serving, close-minded, half-witted (make that quarter-witted) twits who believe in everything I reject, viz. the cruel treatment of farm animals,

GOOD MONEY

the feeding of an inappropriate diet to dogs and cats, lying to consumers and all the rest of it.

I am angry (really, really angry) about the damage that all the big food companies are doing to the environment and their careless disregard for human health, animal health and – most infuriating of all – animal welfare. I am also angry with the media and certain so-called animal welfare charities, which, instead of speaking out against the dreadful injustice being done to other species, endorse and thus effectively participate in it.

It can be damaging to a business if its founders and/or decision-makers express extreme emotions and/or voice strongly held opinions. Show too much feeling, say something that is impolitic, and it can have the effect of turning employees, colleagues, suppliers, customers, supporters and others away from you and your company. Business leaders are expected to be bland, conservative, cautious, measured and diplomatic.

Stuff that.

Don't hide what you think, feel or believe because it may result in the loss of customers or money. The support of those who agree with you will more than compensate you for any loss of custom you experience. However, I would offer a word of warning. Stick to your subject. It ill

240

**DON'T HIDE
WHAT YOU
THINK,
FEEL OR
BELIEVE
JUST BECAUSE
IT MAY RESULT
IN THE LOSS
OF CUSTOMERS
OR MONEY.**

behoves any entrepreneur – ethical or otherwise – to speak out about topics unrelated to his or her area of expertise. Honey's customers will tolerate me talking about dog food, the agri-food sector, the environment, the over-use of antibiotics, blood-farming and anything else that is related to dog food. They won't tolerate me talking about, say, the refugee crisis or the future of Europe.

DO WHAT YOU CAN

THERE is a version of Loren Eiseley's essay 'The Star Thrower' in which two men are walking along a beach covered by thousands of washed-up, dying starfish. One of the men starts throwing individual starfish back into the water. The other man points out that there are so many starfish in trouble nothing his companion can do will make any difference. The first man replies that it will make a difference to each starfish he saves. It is an oft-repeated story but that doesn't make it any the less true.

By any measure you care to choose – economic, financial, environmental, agricultural, political or social – the world is in crisis.

However, no matter how dreadful the situation appears, we are, none of us, powerless. We can

WE KNOW THAT
WE CAN'T PUT
EVERYTHING
WE FEEL
STRONGLY
ABOUT
(AND THERE ARE
A GREAT NUMBER
OF ISSUES WE FEEL
STRONGLY ABOUT)
RIGHT, BUT THERE
ARE THINGS WE
CAN DO, AND IT IS
OUR DUTY
TO TRY TO DO THEM.

———————————

educate ourselves. We can support the causes we believe in. We can lobby. We can protest. We can vote. We can choose how we spend our money. We can choose how we earn our money.

Sydney Smith, the nineteenth-century parson, put it in a nutshell when he said: 'It is the greatest of all mistakes to do nothing because you can only do a little – do what you can.'

We know that we can't put everything we feel strongly about (and there are a great number of issues we feel strongly about) right, but there are things we can do, and it is our duty to try to do them.